A psychologist's guide to anger management

DON'T SHOUT, SPEAK

Express yourself without yelling or causing harm

Ventoop Books

First Edition: July 2024

For more information contact:

contact@startsera.com

startsera.com

Published by Ventoop Books

Cover design by Ventoop Books

ISBN 978-1-80412-004-0

I dedicate this book to all the tender, vulnerable parts of ourselves that are hurting and struggling to express themselves.

Table of Contents

Introduction

Welcome to a journey that promises to change the way you understand and deal with your rage. Let's face it: managing anger can be challenging. You're here because you know that anger, while natural, can sometimes feel like it's running your life. This book is designed to help you take control, but first, let's talk about some common challenges you might encounter along the way.

Is anger always bad? Many of us grow up believing that anger is inherently destructive and should be suppressed, and we often do that. But what if I told you that anger is as natural as laughing at a joke, crying at a sad movie, or jumping at a loud noise, and like all emotions, it serves an important purpose? It alerts us to injustices, boundary violations, and unmet needs. This book will show you how to use that energy positively instead of bottling it up or letting it all out.

We all want quick fixes, especially when dealing with something as intense as anger. It's normal to feel a bit frustrated if you don't see immediate changes. But remember, managing anger is a journey, not a sprint. Small steps lead to big changes, and I will help you celebrate those tiny victories along the way.

Dealing with anger can be tough because our responses become habits, and changing these patterns can feel like an uphill battle. Here, you will find practical strategies to help you recognize and modify these automatic responses. With patience and practice, you'll learn new, healthier, and more constructive ways to respond.

To support this change, I've created a helpful pack with a workbook where you can engage with the material, turning this reading into your guided, personalized journey and a journal to continue self-discovery. You will simply scan the code to download the workbook and journal on the following pages.

Expressing anger can be scary, especially if you're concerned about facing confrontation. You might worry that addressing your anger will lead to conflict. This book offers tools for assertive communication, allowing you to express your feelings clearly and respectfully without damaging the relationships.

Sometimes, it feels like our surroundings are designed to push our buttons. Specific settings can constantly trigger our anger, whether it's a stressful work environment or a chaotic home life. We'll explore ways to influence your environment, set boundaries, and develop coping strategies to manage these unavoidable triggers.

When you're under intense stress or feeling emotionally overloaded, it can be challenging to maintain your composure and manage your anger. In the following chapters, you will discover techniques to help you handle stress and boost your emotional strength to stay calm no matter what comes your way.

Some worry that managing their anger will mean losing control or being taken advantage of. In reality, learning to manage anger is about gaining better control over your emotions and reactions. Here, I will guide you in developing assertive anger management skills that will empower you without compromising your boundaries.

Cultural or familial norms may encourage aggressive behavior as being acceptable. It can be challenging to break away from these deeply rooted beliefs. I encourage you to critically evaluate these norms and adopt healthier, more effective ways of expressing anger.

Do you ever feel angry without knowing why? Identifying what specifically triggers your anger can be tricky. I will give you some exercises and tools to help you identify your triggers and understand where they come from. The workbook and the following journal are amazingly useful for a guided inner understanding.

Sometimes, rage might make us feel powerful or get others to do what we want at the moment. However, these short-term benefits can often lead to long-term costs. In this book, you have different ways to experience these benefits without getting angry, which can help improve your relationships and overall well-being.

Change can be uncomfortable, and it's natural to resist altering your behavior. But remember, the benefits of managing your anger — improved relationships, better health, and greater peace of mind — are well worth the effort. I wrote this book to support you in embracing a growth mindset and encourage you to welcome change as a pathway to inner healing and connection.

While anger can be powerful and overwhelming, it's important not to let it control our actions. Managing anger can be an exciting journey, but it involves bravely confronting vulnerabilities and training your brain to change its reaction to triggers, which, by the end of the book, you will know by heart.

The difference this journey makes is in the way we connect with ourselves, find inner peace, and the impact we have on those around us we love and cherish.

1. The Turmoil Within

Meet Eliot, a talented sculptor whose touch can give stone life. Art is his world, always brimming with admiration and striving for perfection. Eliot's sculptures were more than works of art; they were raw expressions of feelings frozen in time. Each curve and edge whispered tales of fiery passion and profound depth. The drive to be creative wasn't limited to Eliot's work; it consumed every aspect of his life.

There are both good and bad sides to Eliot's passion. It pushed him to be more artistic in a way that words alone couldn't. His works spoke to and touched people. Everyone showed an interest in them because each piece had a lot of feelings. But powerful emotions, like Eliot's, can sometimes come to the surface and show up in strange ways.

In a world where everyone watches everything and sees every flaw, Eliot's passion morphed into anger. This anger doesn't fight crime or bring about change; it hurts people. During an exhibition that should have been the prime point of Eliot's career, he got angry at what he thought was an unfair critique.

The outburst was honest, unfiltered, and open. It was both a moment of weakness and uncontrolled anger. The consequences were immediate and continuous. Once teeming with great opportunities, the art world was halted by his controversial actions that upset many.

Eliot discovered a valuable lesson: his passion built his artistic reputation, but his anger could ruin it without restraint. This turning point sent Eliot on a new journey of insight and understanding. As he reflected, he realized his anger was the driving force behind his actions. It was difficult to accept that the same fire that fueled his art also threatened to consume him.

I chose Eliot's story because it made me reflect on the thin line between anger and passion. His work as a sculptor showcased his profound talent and love for art expression. Still, his destructive outbursts revealed the intensity of his passion and the vulnerability of his artistic vision.

The goal of this journey is to find balance. Eliot's fight to understand and deal with his anger wasn't just to save his career but also to find peace and master this passion without letting it control him.

Anger, a natural emotion

Think of anger as a fiery core nestled deep within us, much like the earth's core — powerful, primal, and sometimes indispensable. This is our body's way of telling us when something is wrong, like when someone belittles or hurts us.

But we should handle anger with care and respect, just like any other natural force. If we don't release the pressure on this heated core, it might erupt with unforeseen consequences.

This dual side of anger is evident in Eliot Reed's story. It makes him more defensive about his work and sparks his creativity. Because of this, he is unconventional, says what he thinks, and fights for his artistic vision. The darker, more dangerous side intensified Eliot's anger, and he feared losing everything he had worked so hard to achieve. It wasn't just about saving his art. His public outburst was a wake-up call, a stark warning of what could happen.

From Eliot's and our own experiences, we learn the critical lesson of the need to understand and manage our anger. It shows us that anger can be our friend but can do much harm if we don't keep it in check.

If you want to control your anger, you don't have to ignore it or push it down. Instead, find healthy ways to talk about your thoughts that don't hurt others or yourself. Start by listening to the signals from that fiery core within, interpreting its messages, and channeling that energy positively rather than aggressively.

Early signs of escalating anger

Have you ever felt peaceful but then sensed a storm gathering inside you?

This tornado doesn't happen by chance. It's a demonstration of the complex relationship that exists between our bodies and our brains, signaling an imminent eruption. My dear friend, the indicators are as varied as the stories written on our hands: for many, it shows up as a sudden heat wave in the face, clenched hands, or words automatically turned into verbal weapons. There was a roar in Eliot's ears, and his vision blurred. These were signs he was losing control, which would destroy his relationships and his reputation.

Read on for a better look at these signs and some valuable tips on how to deal with them.

I. Physical signs

The body has its language, a series of physical cues that tell us a lot about how we're feeling. Getting angry doesn't happen unexpectedly; many changes and reactions in the body show it is emerging. These physical signs aren't just emotions; they come from our evolutionary biology and are remnants of the fight-or-flight response designed to get the body ready to act. Figuring out how to express anger with your body is like learning a new language. We must pay close attention to the subtle ways our bodies speak to us.

1. Increased heart rate

The most noticeable symptom is an accelerated heartbeat that feels like a drumbeat in your chest. This physiological response is part of the body's fight-or-flight mechanism, which prepares you for perceived threats.

Here is what you can do to lower your heart rate:

- Pause and breathe. As simple as it sounds, taking a few deep breaths can help calm a racing heartbeat. Imagine each breath slowing the drumbeat in your chest.

- Channel your energy into physical activity, such as a brisk stroll or a quick set of jumping jacks. It's a productive way to channel that fight-or-flight energy.

2. Tight muscles

Muscles, especially in the jaw, neck, and shoulders, can tense up as part of the body's readiness to respond to danger. This tension can cause discomfort or even pain if it is not addressed. Here are some relaxation tips:

- Gently stretch tense areas in your neck, shoulders, and jaw. It's like telling your body it's safe to lower the drawbridge and relax.

- A heated pad or towel to tense areas can help muscles release tension. It's like sending a signal to your body that it's okay to unwind.

3. Breathing changes

As the body prepares for action, breathing may become faster and shallower. This change in breathing patterns can increase a sense of urgency and anxiety.

To calm down, try the following:

- Practice taking deep, slow breaths. Inhale through your nose, fill your lungs, and exhale slowly through your mouth. It's like taking a deep breath to reduce the intensity of your anger.
- Apps and videos that walk you through breathing exercises can be beneficial. Think of them as a co-pilot, helping you navigate turbulent emotional skies.

4. Feeling hot or flushed

Increased blood flow to the face and upper body can cause feelings of heat and flushing. This physical sign is often a clear warning to others that anger is brewing.

To cool things down a bit, here's what you can do:

- Splash cold water on your face or apply something cool, like a can of soda, to your forehead or the neck area. It's like a quick reboot for your body, triggered by the low temperature.

- Close your eyes and visualize a cool breeze or being in a chilly place. Visualization can have a powerful effect on your body's response.

5. Clenched fists or jaw

Making fists or clenching your mouth is a physical way of getting ready for a fight. Clenching the jaw tightens the facial and neck muscles and prepares the head for impact. This is a holdover from our ancestors' need to protect essential areas during fights, so it's important to notice this tension before it takes hold of you and then:

- Consciously relax. Make a deliberate effort to unclench your fists and relax your jaw. It's like dropping your arms and choosing peace.
- Keep a stress ball or similar object close by. Squeezing allows you to release some pent-up energy without engaging in conflict.

Seeing and dealing with these physical signs of anger prevents your emotions from worsening and teaches you how to handle your anger better. To gain emotional control, it is essential to pay attention to your body's cues and use techniques that help you calm down.

II. Emotional and cognitive signs

People not only feel angry, they also think about it. Cognitive signs of anger reflect how our thoughts form and are shaped by this powerful emotion. These ways of thinking don't just change how we see things at the time; they can also alter how we act and make choices, sometimes leading us to regret or make things worse.

1. Irritability

Minor annoyances can be an early sign of anger because they show you can't cope with things getting frustrating for long. A sign that you're about to get angry is when everything bothers you, like the sound of someone chewing or a door being left open. To stop this emotion from intensifying, you need to:

- *Take a break.* Step away from whatever is bothering you. A brief break can occasionally reset your tolerance levels.

2. Restlessness

Feeling agitated and too impatient to sit still can be a subtle but telling sign that anger is bubbling under the surface, looking for a way to express itself. This restlessness is more than just physical discomfort; it's an emotional signal, an internal alarm system that warns you that something in your emotional landscape is out of balance. You can do the following in these moments:

- *Turn that restlessness into physical activity.* Going for a run, practicing yoga, or even doing household chores like vacuuming, washing dishes, or tidying up can help you.

- Alternatively, *engage in creative activities* such as drawing, writing, or playing music that provide a constructive outlet for your pent-up energy.

3. *Anxiety or nervousness*

The fear of what will happen if we express our fury often accompanies feelings of anger. You might be afraid of how other people will see you, how it will affect your relationships, or whether you can hold your temper once you yell. Keeping your anger in check can cause anxiety, and then the anxiety can make it even harder to face and release your anger healthily.

People who have been taught that anger is terrible or have had negative experiences expressing rage may struggle with internal conflict. The fear is not just about the immediate consequences but also about deeper fears of rejection, losing control, or harming others physically or emotionally. To prevent and change that pattern, do the following:

- *Talk it out.* Share your feelings with someone close to you. Opening up to a trusted friend can help lessen the intensity of your emotions.

Relaxation techniques like deep breathing or progressive muscle relaxation (PMR) can significantly reduce stress, anxiety, and anger.

- *Deep breathing* involves focusing on slow, deliberate breaths. Breathing deeply from the belly helps get as much fresh air into the lungs as possible, which increases oxygen flow and helps reduce tension and stress.

- *PMR* is a technique in which each muscle group in the body is tensioned, but not to the point of strain, and then slowly relaxed. Start with your feet and work up to your face, or vice versa. Tense each muscle group for about five seconds, then relax for 30 seconds and notice the sensation. Try to keep your focus on your body.

4. *Intrusive thoughts*

It's a clear sign you may become enraged if you can't stop thinking about a situation or a person who made you angry. This mental replay, whether dwelling on a comment someone made or constantly going over a frustrating situation, will worsen your anger.

If you do nothing, these thoughts can turn into full-blown anger any moment after they are planted in your mind. The more you think about them, the more mental energy they consume. This makes you more emotionally aroused, which gets you ready to be angry.

Thoughts that won't go away often tell a story of unfairness or wrongdoing, whether real or imagined. In your mind, you might keep building and rebuilding arguments, thinking of everything you wish you had said, or imagining different outcomes where you win. Sometimes, this mental exercise makes you feel you're regaining control or preparing for future conflicts, but in reality, it just keeps you stuck in a cycle of anger and negativity. The more something is repeated, the stronger and hotter the feeling becomes. You can prevent that by doing the following:

- *Push the thoughts around.* Think about how accurate or helpful these thoughts are. If they're based on facts, what are they? Putting your unwanted thoughts to the test can help lessen their effect.
- *Keep yourself busy.* Do something to distract yourself from these thoughts, like drawing, writing, or household chores. When you take your mind off the cycle, you can sometimes see things more clearly when you return to them later.

5. *Feeling overwhelmed*

Sometimes, when things don't seem just right, we feel powerless and frustrated at the same time. One important sign that anger is brewing is when you start feeling overwhelmed and like you're about to lose control.

When we encounter unfairness in our daily lives, at work, or in society, we wonder if the world is fair and just. Even though we try our best, it's tough to accept that things can go wrong for us or others. It's natural to feel vulnerable when we realize we have little control over a situation. This can make us feel like the ground is shifting beneath our feet, and we are losing control, which can be overwhelming.

Often, when we go from feeling stressed to angry, it happens pretty quickly. When we witness injustice, our natural instinct is to restore fairness and take back control. This type of anger can initially feel empowering — like a fiery response aiming to confront injustice and regain control. While it's normal to experience these emotions, they can sometimes lead us away from finding a solution and into conflict.

When feeling overwhelmed, do the following:

- *Pay attention to how you feel.* Know that being stressed is normal and doesn't mean you can't do anything. Recognizing and accepting your feelings without judgment can help you better deal with them.
- After that, try to see things from *different points of view.* Take a closer look at things that appear to be wrong at first. Every detail matters.
- Remember to focus on the aspects of the situation that *you have the power to influence.* This might involve discussing what's unfair, advocating for change, or finding ways to support yourself and others who are impacted by the situation.
- *Assign tasks and set priorities.* Whenever you can, consider delegating some of your tasks to others. Receiving assistance or sharing the workload can help make things more manageable.

III. Behavioral signs

These are the outward signs of our emotions and how our ideas, feelings, and attitudes appear in our bodies. They can be very subtle or obvious, like a quick change in body language, facial expression, or even long-term patterns of interacting with each other. These signs are the breadcrumbs that lead us back to our emotional selves, offering clues to what we are experiencing but may not yet have the words to express.

1. Raised voice:

An increased voice volume is often one of the most immediate and recognizable signs of anger. It's a physical manifestation of the body's fight-or-flight response, where the intensity of our emotions makes our voices louder than usual.

This increase in volume may be an unconscious attempt to assert dominance, demand attention, or express a sense of urgency or frustration. But while it may feel like a release of pent-up energy, a raised voice can escalate tensions and make it harder for others to respond constructively. Instead, follow these steps:

- *Pause and assess.* Notice when your voice starts to rise and use it as a signal to pause. Ask yourself, "What am I really upset about?"
- *Deliberately lower the volume.* Actively work on lowering your voice. It may feel strange initially, but lowering your

volume can help reduce the emotional intensity for you and the person you're talking to.

2. Sarcasm or cynicism

Sarcasm and cynicism can be more subtle indicators of anger and are often used to express dissatisfaction without confrontation. Sarcasm, with its sharp wit, can mask anger with humor, making it a double-edged sword that cuts through dialogue and potentially hurts the recipient.

Cynicism is a deep-seated distrust or pessimism, often stemming from unresolved anger or disappointment.

While both can serve as protective mechanisms, shielding us from showing vulnerability, they can also alienate others and prevent genuine connection. When using these masks, here are a few things you could try:

- *Identify the feeling.* Before you use sarcasm, try to recognize your underlying emotion. Are you hurt? Disappointed? Misunderstood? Disrespected?
- *Express it honestly.* Instead of hiding behind sarcasm, try to express it directly but politely. For example, you might say, "*I feel left out of the decision-making process, and that's upsetting to me.*"

3. Isolation

When we choose to isolate, it means that anger is directed inwardly. This behavioral response may be driven by a wish to avoid conflict, a fear of expressing anger, or a feeling of helplessness in changing our situation. When we respond to anger with isolation, it can lead to a cycle of rumination, trapping us in a loop of relentless, angry thoughts. While time alone can allow us to reflect on ourselves, being isolated for too long can make us feel more enraged and disconnected from the support and candidness crucial for emotional healing.

If you find yourself withdrawing from others, it might be a sign that you're holding in your anger. This can have adverse effects similar to outward aggression. Remember:

- It's okay to take some intentional time alone. Dedicate this period to *increasing your emotional awareness* and reflecting on your feelings as a positive choice rather than a way to avoid dealing with them.
- *Seek reconnection*. After reflecting on yourself, consider reaching out to others to reconnect. You could start by having a lighthearted conversation about something unrelated to what's been bothering you. This can be a great way to break free from feelings of isolation.

4. Pacing or fidgeting

When anger seeks an outlet, it often creates a sense of discomfort in our bodies. You may notice your foot tapping incessantly, your fingers drumming on the table, or a general inability to find a comfortable position.

These physical manifestations are your body's response to the unresolved pent-up energy that anger creates, saying, "Hey, we need to deal with this," urging you to acknowledge and address whatever is causing it.

To effectively deal with the underlying issue, it's important to:

- Engage in mindfulness or grounding exercises to *anchor yourself in the present moment.* Focus on sensations such as the feel of your feet on the ground or the rhythm of your breathing.
- Or find a constructive way to *channel that energy.* Exercise, dancing, and even cleaning can help release tension.

These behavioral gestures show anger and a desire for understanding, compassion, and constructive action. When we notice these signs in ourselves and others, we can take steps to address the main reasons for our rage. This can lead to better communication, self-awareness, and healthier ways to handle our emotions.

The deep volcano

Returning to Eliot's world, we encounter a scenario familiar to many professionals: a high-stakes environment with intense demands and no place for mistakes. Imagine a landscape dominated by looming deadlines that resemble towering cliffs, swirling criticism like relentless winds, and sky-high expectations. For Eliot, this wasn't just the setting of his life; it was the atmosphere he breathed, laden with demands and pressures that could test the resilience of the stoutest of hearts. Sound familiar?

A constant series of challenges and criticisms fueled Eliot's frustration and anger. Each obstacle, no matter its size, fueled an already blazing inferno.

This accumulation of stressors is reminiscent of the geological forces at work beneath a volcano, where layers of ash and magma build up and create immense pressure. Similarly, Eliot's frustrations and perceived slights accumulated, creating a threatening internal force. Each incident increased the pressure. Criticism, whether constructive or caustic, acted like gusts of wind fanning the flames. Eliot's explosive outburst wasn't the result of a single event but the culmination of multiple pressures — personal, professional, and emotional — that had reached a critical point. While shocking, this eruption served as a crucial wake-up call for Eliot.

For anyone facing similar pressures, Eliot's story is an excellent reminder that even though the world puts a lot of pressure on us to live up to its standards, it's essential to have ways to handle and ease that pressure; that is critical for keeping a good balance and avoiding these volcanic moments. This book guides you through that process, so continue reading.

Stormy seas

Imagine Eliot at a significant crossroads, like standing in the heart of a bustling city, contemplating which path to take. Despite his successful career, his recent outburst casts a long shadow over his talents.

And then there's his personal life, filled with relationships that his anger may have strained or damaged. Now, he faces a critical question that may resonate with you: Can we truly tame the raging volcano within, or must we prepare for the inevitability of a major eruption?

Eliot's journey from here is more than a struggle with himself. It's a deep exploration of fears, needs, and habits, delving into understanding anger and how to manage it, as it can be powerful and disheartening, but it shouldn't dictate his actions.

What ignites the flare-ups? How can he recognize the early warning signs before an outburst? And most importantly, how can he channel this fiery energy positively and constructively instead of letting it wreak havoc and create chaos?

This journey is full of lessons for Eliot and anyone who

has felt the inner heat of anger rising. It reminds us that mastering our inner storm can be challenging but far from impossible. On this path, we may discover a lot about ourselves, our strengths, and how to transform what may appear to be a weakness into one of our greatest strengths.

Stages of anger

As our understanding of anger improves, we see it as a journey up a mountain. This journey has several stages: beginning at the bottom, ascending, reaching the peak, descending, and finally pausing for a rest. There are five stages of anger: trigger, escalation, crisis, recovery, and depression. We'll go through each stage.

1. Trigger: The journey begins

A trigger is a term used to describe something that provokes anger. This could be a comment, an action, or a memory. Our pasts, beliefs, and emotions shape our unique triggers. Discovering your triggers is like identifying potential roadblocks on your journey. Figuring out what's making you angry is the first thing you need to do to control it.

2. Escalation: The climb

When we escalate, our feelings surge, amplifying the intensity of our emotional experience. For example, when you walk uphill, each step makes your legs and breathing harder.

Feelings of heat or stress and a faster heart rate mark this stage as we move from mild irritation to full-blown anger. It's imperative to step in with techniques like deep breathing, stopping, and refocusing your thoughts that work very well. Remember, you're going uphill and can decide to slow down before you reach the top.

3. Crisis: The peak

The intensity of anger is at its maximum right now. Some actions that may occur include yelling, engaging in violence, or making impulsive choices. At this moment, intense emotions can overpower rational thinking and make focusing difficult. It is crucial to acknowledge this high point because it's the perfect time to use de-escalation techniques, like distancing from the situation until you can calm down.

4. Recovery: Coming down the mountain

When the anger fades away, that's when the healing process can truly begin. It's the part of the hike where you get off the mountain and ponder what happened, think more clearly, and contemplate the consequences of your anger. At this stage, it is common to feel the need to apologize or try to make amends for actions taken in anger.

5. Depression: The rest

After things settle down, many of us may feel a bit down or blue. We might wish we handled things differently and started to see where our anger came from. It's kind of like feeling exhausted after a strenuous hike. It's an excellent time to think about what set off our emotions and what it says about our needs and fears. This reflection can help us figure out how to handle similar situations in a healthier way.

Remembering these stages helps us understand that anger follows a path like any journey. If we know what might cause anger, we can prepare to handle those situations more calmly. When we feel anger escalating, we can take a moment to calm down before things get out of control. Staying present and mindful during the peak of our anger can help us avoid reacting impulsively, leading to a smoother experience. Going through the recovery phase and beyond allows us to reflect, learn, and become emotionally stronger while improving our ability to manage our temper. Understanding each stage can help us handle anger, recognize triggers, prevent escalation, and safely manage intense emotions.

Discover the stages of your anger

After reading Chapter 1 and thinking about how Eliot's anger and emotion played off of each other, let's take a moment to reflect. While here, think about a recent event that made you feel intensely passionate and angry. Consider how these emotions impacted your actions and what lessons you took from them. I use this list of questions to help my clients explore their inner selves. Let's answer these questions to start our trip, just like Eliot had to learn to handle his inner fire.

1. *Identify your volcano.* Reflect on something that has recently made you upset. What made you feel like this?

2. *Recognize the signs.* Think about how your body and mind react when you're mad. When you get angry, do you notice changes in how you feel, think, or act?

3. *Explore the impact.* Consider how your anger impacts those around you. When did your anger get in the way of a relationship, a job at work, or a personal relationship? How did it feel afterward?

4. *Understand the source.* Find out more about what's making you furious. Do you often get angry because you feel misunderstood, undervalued, or disrespected, like Eliot?

5. *Evaluate the aftermath.* How do you usually make peace with yourself and others after getting angry or showing rage? How tough is it for you to move on from anger?

Don't worry if you can't answer all of these questions right now. They're here to get you thinking about how you deal with anger and help you prepare for the journey ahead.

 You can also start by doing this exciting quiz in the workbook to see how much you know about anger management. Simply scan the code to get the workbook.

By the end of the book, you'll know your triggers, learn what makes you mad, have many tools you can use immediately, and see your relationships bloom.

THE UNBRIDLED STORM

2. Gloomy Skies Ahead

Have you ever noticed how water boils over the moment you look away? It's a lot like anger, which simmers unseen until it suddenly overflows. Quietly seething beneath the surface, it can go unnoticed until it unexpectedly boils over, resulting in a messy situation. This chapter will help you catch that simmer before it explodes, spot those anger bubbles, understand what's causing the heat, and learn some neat tricks to cool things down.

Healthy vs. unhealthy anger

Yes, it's true — anger can be constructive in certain situations! Think of anger as a tool in your emotional toolbox.

Like any tool, its effectiveness depends on how you use it. Let's break down what makes anger healthy and when it becomes unhealthy.

Healthy anger: The constructive tool

Healthy anger may seem counterintuitive at first. After all, isn't anger supposed to be a negative emotion? If you recall from the first few pages, I mentioned that anger, like all emotions, serves an important purpose. It alerts us to injustices, boundary violations, and our own needs that may not be met. The way we handle and communicate our anger is crucial in determining whether it becomes a constructive or destructive force in our lives. Let's examine the traits of healthy anger to grasp better how it can serve as a catalyst for positive transformation.

- *Controlled.*

Imagine you're holding the reins of a horse, gently guiding it along the path. This is a perfect metaphor for temperate anger. You feel the emotion, acknowledge its presence, and decide where to direct it. You're in charge, not the anger. This control prevents the emotion from escalating into rage or leading to actions you may later regret. Feeling the heat of anger, but using it to warm you up enough to see clearly, not to burn down the house. You're experiencing anger but managing it, not the other way around.

- Healthy anger is *communicative.*

It's the difference between a tirade that leaves destruction in its wake and a clear, assertive message articulating your feelings, needs, and boundaries. Communicating anger healthily means using "I" statements that focus on your experience rather than blaming or attacking the other person. For example, say, "I get frustrated when I'm not heard because it makes me feel undervalued," rather than, "You never listen to me!" This approach opens the door to understanding and resolution rather than conflict.

- The essence of healthy anger is that it is *constructive.*

Rather than dwelling on the problem, healthy anger seeks solutions. It's like fixing a broken step that trips you up when you step on it rather than cursing it every time you stumble. Healthy anger can inspire us to address the underlying cause of our frustration and take action to avoid similar problems in the future, channeling the energy of anger into actions that improve situations, relationships, and personal well-being.

- One of the most important aspects of healthy anger is that it is *temporary.*

Like rain in the morning that clears up in the afternoon, healthy anger arises, fulfills its role, and then fades. It doesn't linger or turn into resentment. Once we acknowledge, express, and act constructively, it fades away, leaving room for other emotions and states of being. The temporary nature of anger ensures that it doesn't have complete control over our feelings; instead, it is just one of our many emotions that shape our inner experiences.

Unhealthy anger: The destructive force

When anger becomes unhealthy, it can harm the person experiencing it and their relationships. It can completely control one's thoughts and make one act in ways that can have lasting consequences. We need to look closer at the signs of unhealthy anger and understand why it's necessary to identify and address it.

- *Out of control.*

When anger takes over, it's like not having an anchor and getting caught in a storm. Depending on how strong your feelings are, you may find that you act without giving them much thought. This lack of control can make you say harmful things, act aggressively, or make choices that you will deeply regret. Your anger is in charge, and you're just along for the ride. This can hurt relationships, make you feel bad, and even have legal or professional consequences.

- *Hurtful.*

A need to hurt is often a sign of unhealthy anger. When people want to blame, criticize, or put down others, their words become weapons. They don't solve the problem at hand and make things worse. Such angry outbursts can do a lot of damage to relationships by breaking trust and leaving mental scars. Unhealthy anger is harmful and can leave marks on the person who feels it and the one who receives it, making it harder to get along and heal.

- *Lasting.*

Good anger goes away when its cause is dealt with, but unhealthy anger lasts longer. It's like leaving a pot on the stove for too long; the pressure and heat build-up until the pot is about to spill over. When the root cause of anger isn't addressed, it can resurface repeatedly, even for trivial reasons. With time, this can become chronic anger, where the person is constantly irritable and hostile. This harms their health and quality of life.

- *Disruptive.*

The very nature of unhealthy anger is to cause trouble. It doesn't stay inside the person; it spreads to other parts of their life and changes them. When loved ones fear making someone angry, their relationships can suffer. Anger can disrupt work life by causing disagreements or making rash judgments. Chronic anger is linked to several health problems, such as high blood pressure and heart disease, and mental health problems, such as anxiety and sadness. The negative consequences of unhealthy anger show how important it is to deal with and healthily share these feelings.

Identifying and differentiating between the two

During a stressful situation, telling the difference

between healthy and unhealthy anger can be as challenging as not having glasses to read small print. Here are some practical insights to help you identify and differentiate between the two types of anger when emotions run high.

Take a step back!

Putting this off is the first thing you must do to clear your mind about what made you angry (trigger) and your response. This break is beneficial; it gives your brain a chance to use its higher-level thought skills and calm down. Here's the right way to use this pause and make it effective:

"What is my goal here? Deal with it amicably or seek revenge?"

Asking yourself this question helps to clarify your intentions. If you aim to get back at them, you're probably getting into unhealthy anger territory. This is when you focus on "winning" the argument at the cost of the friendship.

It's healthy and constructive to channel your anger toward finding a solution that considers both sides' needs and feelings.

"Am I in control of my anger, or is my anger in control?"

This question is about determining who is in charge. If you feel you can't stop your anger from controlling what you say and do, then your anger has gone too far and into unhealthy territory. When you express anger in a healthy way, you're in charge and not letting it take over your behavior.

"Will this matter in a week, a month, or a year?"

Perspective is a powerful tool. Imagine how this situation may play out in the future and consider how important it is. That should help you determine if your anger is justified. In the big picture, this question can help you determine if the situation calls for a strong emotional reaction or if it's something you can let go of.

Understanding the difference between healthy and unhealthy anger empowers you to control your reactions in crises and transform anger from a potential enemy into a helpful ally that guides you toward fairness, respect, and constructive outcomes.

Inner sparks of simmering anger

Think about those days when it feels like everything is against you: the alarm doesn't go off, traffic is a nightmare, or someone cuts in front of you. Maybe it's something more profound, like feeling unnoticed about your efforts or wrestling with doubts about your abilities. These moments flame under your emotional pot, slowly boiling your anger.

We all have personal triggers that gradually turn up the heat. It could be a disagreement that hasn't been resolved or something more profound, like a fear of missing out or memories of challenging times.

These aren't just annoyances; they are signals of deeper sources of anger related to personal insecurities, past experiences, unmet expectations, stress, communication problems, physical discomfort, environmental factors, or challenged values.

To fully understand what can heighten our emotions, we must closely examine these triggers.

I. Personal insecurities

Our insecurities are like hidden fault lines that affect how we see ourselves, our relationships, our looks, and what we've done well. When these fears are provoked, it can feel like a sudden earthquake, and anger can quickly come in to protect our inner selves.

Rage acts like a guard, yelling loudly to protect our self-esteem and parts of our self-image that make us feel vulnerable. It's like our internal guard dog barks when we feel weak, when someone casually criticizes our work, or when we compare to others on social media.

Dealing with our fears when we're angry and want to protect ourselves might seem easier and less scary. It's like putting on armor — we might feel better, but it's heavy and can make it hard to move around or connect deeply with others.

Now that we're aware, we have the power to change

this trend. Instead of using anger as a shield, we can work on our insecurities. Taking this approach will make us more open and less defensive in our responses. To begin, here are some steps to follow:

1. *Start with self-reflection.*

First, like an archeologist, you need to dig deep into your feelings to determine exactly what makes you angry. Is it when other people criticize you or when you compare yourself to someone else? These moments often show us how insecure we are. Grab a journal and start writing. Just by doing this one thing, you can gain valuable insight into the patterns and hidden insecurities behind your anger.

2. *Use positive affirmations.*

Because of our natural desires to stay alive, our brains are pattern-seeking machines that tend to focus on the bad. Saying positive affirmations to yourself is a powerful way to break this habit. Write affirmations that give voice to your inner you, like "I am motivated and will succeed" or "If they can, I am capable and can do this too."

Repeat these every day, but especially when you're having doubts. With time, this method can help you change your focus from your weaknesses to your strengths.

3. *Ask for help.*

Talking about our fears can be scary, but it's

necessary to conquer them. You could share with your family and friends or consider seeing a psychologist. Expressing your worries and fears makes them less powerful and brings you closer to everyone who feels vulnerable. People who have been through the same things as you are likely to relate, understand, and help you.

4. *Practice self-compassion*

Treat yourself with the kindness and patience you would show a close friend. Understand that everyone has flaws and makes mistakes; it doesn't diminish your worth. When you are self-critical, stop and ask, "Would I talk to someone I love this way?" Shifting towards self-compassion can bring about a significant transformation in your self-perception and how you deal with insecurities.

5. *Challenge yourself.*

Growth occurs when we venture outside of our comfort zones. Find the things that your fears are stopping you from doing, and give yourself small, doable goals. If you're having trouble with your appearance, try a new exercise focusing on health and strength instead of looks. If your insecurities get in the way of your work goals, set small goals and celebrate each. The challenges you face and the wins you achieve can boost your confidence and sense of self-worth.

Changing long-held fears doesn't happen overnight.

So be patient, persistent, and ready to face hard facts about yourself. You'll find that what used to hold you back can now be your most fantastic opportunity for growth and strength as you progress. This doesn't imply that you will never experience anger again, but you will not allow anger to control your reactions.

II. Historical triggers

Going through trauma, abuse, or deep mental pain leaves invisible scars that time can't erase on its own. Dormant within us, our concealed wounds awaken when confronted with reminders of the past, reigniting the pain we once felt. These historical triggers don't just bring back memories; they make us feel something deep inside, which is often fury. However, this anger is not simply an emotion but a commitment to never feel powerless again.

Expressing our rage is like building a protective wall that shows we're in control of a harsh world.

Understanding the source of our anger is imperative for transforming impulsive reactions into intentional behavior. Here are some useful ways to deal with and fix these deep-seated triggers:

1. Acknowledge and validate your feelings

It's okay to feel the way you do, and it's okay to feel angry about what happened. Accepting this releases you and reminds you that you deserve better, making healing easier.

Keep a journal of times when you feel triggered. Writing can be a helpful tool in understanding and accepting your thoughts and feelings. Pause and contemplate the content you've written to better understand your past and present feelings. Include statements like "*I felt ……. I know my feelings are valid*" or "*I still am feeling……….. It's okay to still feel that way about what happened*" to help you remember.

2. Identify your triggers

Figure out precisely what is making you angry. Is it related to speech, environment, or time? Knowing what sets off your responses, you can better prepare and handle them.

It's helpful to keep a record of times when you feel angry or upset unintentionally. Notice what happened, who was there, and what was said or done. With time, you'll see trends that show what triggers you. Practicing mindfulness can help you better understand your emotions in the present.

3. Seek professional support

Trauma and deep emotional pain are challenging to deal with alone. With professional help, you can figure out how to cope with these events and lessen their effect on you. Look for therapists who specialize in trauma-informed care or cognitive-behavioral therapy. Or, you could join a support group for people who have been through the same kind of trauma. Talking about your burdens in a protected setting can provide wholehearted support.

4. Practice grounding techniques

Grounding methods can help you stay focused on the present when past triggers arise. Techniques from mindfulness like deep breathing and tactile exercises (such as holding a cold object or focusing on the details of an object) can be helpful.

- *Try the 5-4-3-2-1 technique.* Name 5 things you can see, 4 you can touch, 3 you can hear, 2 you can smell, and 1 you can taste. This will bring your focus to the present.

- Or do this *deep breathing exercise, the 4-7-8 technique*, to calm your nervous system when triggered. Place the tip of your tongue against the ridge of tissue just behind your upper front teeth and keep it there throughout the exercise. Begin by exhaling all the air in your lungs through your mouth and inhaling gently through your nose to a mental count of 4. Hold your breath for a count of 7. Exhale completely through your mouth to the count of 8. This completes one cycle. Repeat the cycle three more times.

5. Create new narratives

It's important to focus on writing stories that reflect your strength and resilience. You've encountered and overcome challenging situations, and while survival was the priority, now is the time to use the strength from those experiences for personal growth.

Describe an event in the past that made you mad. Rewrite the story from a perspective that showcases your ability to bounce back and overcome challenges. This will be your updated ending from now on. Embrace your transformation and believe in yourself.

6. Set boundaries

By setting healthy boundaries, you can exercise positive control over your life, proactively avoid potential triggers, and cultivate healthier relationships.

Clearly state what you won't do. If you practice setting limits assertively rather than aggressively, you'll be able to find time to relax and attend to your well-being.

7. Build a supportive network

Surround yourself with people who support and understand your healing journey. Being part of a supportive community can provide comfort and minimize the impact of triggers.

Choose wisely with whom you share your triggers and past experiences. Make sure these people are empathetic and supportive. Getting involved in community activities or groups that align with your interests or healing journey will make you feel like you belong and have someone to lean on.

Recovering from past traumas and lessening their

impact on anger takes time, courage, and self-kindness. Remember, you have the power to change your future actions, but not what has already occurred in the past. With each small step you take, you'll be closer to finding inner peace and empowerment.

III. Unmet expectations

Expectations — whether our own or those we place on others — often simmer beneath the surface as hidden sources of anger. The gap between what we hope for and reality, whether in personal relationships, career goals, or daily interactions, fuels the flames of frustration and anger.

Picture an ideal day: sunshine upon waking, the perfect cup of coffee, and smooth traffic. Then reality hits: rain drenches you, your coffee spills, and you get stuck in traffic. It's like planning the perfect picnic only to find ants invading. The difference between our dreams and reality can make us feel frustrated and angry.

But it's not just the small stuff; this dynamic also plays out on larger stages. You can aim high in your professional life, anticipating promotions or successful project outcomes, and hope for support, understanding, or agreement from loved ones on important matters, and it doesn't happen. When outcomes don't meet our expectations, disappointment can quickly become anger. It feels like a road with surprises instead of a smooth journey.

Why do expectations trip us up?

Our hopes often look like daydreams, sketches of how we want things to turn out. The trouble begins when we cling too tightly to these fantasies and overlook the complexity and messiness of real life.

Failing to share our expectations can lead to misunderstandings. It's like being upset because someone didn't follow the script in your head. Without clear communication, it's unfair to hold others to unseen standards.

Unrealistic expectations for ourselves and others will always lead to frustration. Having big goals is great, but setting impossible standards leads to disappointment.

So how do we do this? How do we keep our expectations from turning into frustration and then anger?

- *Check in with reality.*

Periodically assess how your expectations compare to actual results. Identifying significant gaps helps you realign your hopes with what's realistically achievable.

- *Talk about it.*

When expectations involve others, communication is key. Discuss your hopes and listen to their perspectives to ensure everyone is on the same page.

- *Be kind to yourself.*

Not achieving every goal is not failure; perfection is not the purpose of life; learning and growing are.

43

- *Flexibility is key.*

View expectations as flexible guidelines, not rigid rules. Life is unpredictable, and being open to surprises can lead to joy and opportunities you didn't hope for. If we start paying attention to what we assume and dealing with it wisely, we can reduce our anger and frustration.

IV. Stress and overwhelm

Too much stress from work, family, or social obligations can make us more likely to become angry. When we're overwhelmed, slight annoyances can appear as significant issues, causing us to overreact.

Think of your patience as a giant rubber band. Daily pressures from work, family, or social interactions gradually stretch it. Although this rubber band is flexible, its resilience is tested as we add more tasks, responsibilities, and stress that do not allow it to return to its original shape. It becomes overstretched, and even a slight tug can cause it to snap.

It's similar to the effects of long-term stress. Our patience is running low, so even insignificant problems become prominent.

You're barely keeping up if you have a lot on your plate, like work, family, and social commitments. Then something goes wrong — you spill coffee on yourself, or someone cuts you off in traffic. These would usually be minor annoyances, but since your patience is already stretched thin, your reaction is much stronger. The coffee spill or traffic incident becomes the final trigger, releasing pent-up stress, frustration, and anger.

Why does this happen?
- *Stress overload.*

Constant stress makes our bodies stay alert, leading to fast reactions even without fully processing what's happening. It's our body's signal that it's overwhelmed and can't focus on analyzing things.

- *Energy drain.*

The constant experience of stress exhausts our energy reserves, leaving us with diminished patience and resilience to confront additional irritations or difficulties. It's like running on empty.

What can we do?
- *Take breaks.*

Much like a rubber band needs to snap back into its original shape, we also need time to recover. Find moments throughout the day to take brief breaks, whether stepping outside for a few minutes or enjoying a cup of coffee or tea.

- *Prioritize.*

Look at everything you're trying to handle and ask yourself, "What really matters?" It's okay to let go of less critical tasks to reduce stress.

- *Learn to say no.*

While it can be challenging, saying no is a necessary skill. It helps you avoid pushing your patience too far, keeps stress under control, and safeguards your inner peace.

- *Find stress relievers.*

Engage in activities that help you relax and reduce stress, such as exercising, reading, taking a walk, or spending time with loved ones. These are calming getaways for your strained patience. Understanding the impact of chronic stress on our anger and learning coping mechanisms can prevent us from reacting explosively to stressful situations. It's essential to take time to relax, recharge, and approach life's slight setbacks with a calm mindset. Keep in mind that the real problem goes beyond the spilled coffee or the traffic jam; it's how much pressure we're under when these things happen. It's time to give ourselves and our rubber bands a well-deserved rest.

V. Communication breakdowns

Misunderstandings, perceived slights, and feelings of being ignored or misheard can lead to angry reactions. A communication breakdown can trigger rage, making us feel ignored, disrespected, or isolated.

When playing telephone, have you ever noticed how humorously a whispered message becomes distorted when it reaches the last player? In a game, it's funny, but not in real life, particularly with our feelings or significant issues. Misunderstandings can be frustrating.

It feels like a real-life game of telephone gone wrong when our messages are ignored or misunderstood. Your friend might think you forgot her birthday if she didn't receive your text, or your boss might misread the tone of an email. These situations, or the mere feeling of not being listened to, can intensify anger.

Being misunderstood or ignored can lead to loneliness, as if our words echo back without acknowledgment. This sense of isolation, of not being seen or valued, can turn tiny sparks of frustration into great flames of rage.

So, how do we avoid these pitfalls? Talk to each other!

It is both simple and complicated. Effective communication can help people connect.

We can understand each other better and communicate effectively when we filter out the confusion and complications.

Yes, communication is the name of the game here. For honest and open dialog, consider the following:

- *Actively listen.*

It takes more than just waiting for your turn to speak. Treating your favorite song as more than just background noise and instead fully immersing yourself in it is akin to actively listening to someone, asking for clarification when needed, and showing genuine interest.

• *Clarify and confirm.*

Make sure you are clear. A fantastic approach is to double-check and clarify any potential confusion or misunderstandings. "Just to make sure I've got this right..." is an effective way to start.

• *Express yourself clearly.*

Communicate as clearly as possible, avoiding ambiguities or leaving out essential details. Think of it as giving directions to someone unfamiliar with your neighborhood. You wouldn't leave out important turns, right?

• *Be open to feedback.*

One of the biggest challenges in communication is admitting that you might be wrong. It might change your views and bring new ones; that's why we should value feedback for our development, but receiving it can be challenging.

Excellent communication is like a refreshing stream that nourishes everything it touches. It allows us to understand each other, manage expectations, and resolve conflicts before they escalate.

Taking the time to listen and understand one another makes us feel valued and respected. This paves the way for better connections and less frustration.

Let's keep an open mind and see disagreements as chances to learn from each other.

VI. Physical discomfort

Physical discomforts, such as hunger, tiredness, or sickness, can significantly impact our emotional well-being, even if we ignore them. Dealing with any of these discomforts can seriously wear down our patience and stress tolerance, leading to unnecessary anger over insignificant things.

Have you ever noticed how being hungry or tired can make slight inconveniences seem big? When you're hungry, picking between pizza and pasta is a challenge. Even the ticking of a clock can be bothersome when you're tired. It's incredible how our bodies can influence our reactions to what's happening around us.

Like a car, your body runs smoothly when it's taken care of and has fuel. It performs poorly when empty or not taken care of for long. Our patience wears thin, and our fuse shortens. This isn't just an old wives' tale; there's science to back it up. Food fuels our bodies, and feeling tired hinders our ability to cope with stress or make wise choices.

And when we're sick? Have you ever noticed that you have zero patience for anything? When unwell, your body uses most of its energy to recover, leaving less for stress or others' needs.

So, what can we do about it?
- *Do not ignore your body's signals* when hungry, tired, or sick. It's like noticing the warning lights on your car's

dashboard and taking it to the service for necessary repairs.

- *Fuel up smartly.* Having a stash of healthy snacks is as important as keeping your car fueled with a suitable gas.
- *Rest and recharge* by getting sufficient sleep and taking regular breaks. It's like getting your car serviced to improve its performance.
- *Take care when you're sick.* Allow yourself to rest. It's okay not to be 100% all the time.

Our emotional mechanisms function more effectively when we attend to our basic physical needs. It's about preparing ourselves to handle life's unexpected challenges calmly. When bothered by little things, pause and ask yourself how you're doing. Sometimes, a quick snack or a brief break is all it takes to reset your emotional balance.

VII. Environmental factors

Environmental triggers like jammed or noisy spaces can heighten our anger. Have you ever been in an overly crowded place, like a big sale or a packed concert, and felt your anxiety rise? Or maybe you've tried to talk to someone in a noisy restaurant but couldn't hear yourself think. Even the slightest noise or disturbance seems to increase your stress levels. This overwhelming feeling is a classic case of sensory overload, which can instantly make us furious.

The things around us have a significant impact on how we feel. Getting annoyed can happen fast with too much noise, too many people, or even an uncomfortable chair. Our environment stresses us out in ways we can't see and makes us irritable for no apparent reason. It's like the challenge of maintaining focus when a fly is buzzing around your room. It might be annoying initially, but it can turn into full-on anger if it keeps happening.

That's what happens to us in stressful situations: not always the problems themselves that bother us, but how they add up over time.

So, how do we keep our cool amid these challenges?

- *Awareness is key.*

  Begin by recognizing the environments that make you uncomfortable. Whether it's noise or crowds, understanding your triggers can help you prepare for or avoid them.

- *Take a breather.*

  Feeling overwhelmed? Give yourself a little space. Simply stepping outside or finding a calm room for a few minutes can significantly reduce your stress levels.

- *Use your senses.*

  Focus on something relaxing. You could listen to a calming song, check out a serene picture on your phone, or take a soothing scent. Concentrating on a particular sensory experience can effectively deal with sensory overload.

- *Plan.*

If you know you will be in a situation that might get too much for you, ensure you have some strategies at hand. Choose a quiet place to escape when you need a break, or set a time limit on how long you'll stay.

- *Practice relaxation techniques.*

Learning quick stress-relief techniques, such as deep breathing or visualization, can be extremely helpful. You can do it almost anywhere, even in a crowded room.

Understanding how your surroundings affect your stress and anger helps you cope and find little ways to chill, even when everything seems super intense. With some planning and practice, you can handle stressful situations and find peace even in the craziest times.

VIII. Values being challenged

When our core values or beliefs are challenged, we tend to get defensive and sometimes angry. This kind of trigger often happens during intense debates or discussions when someone feels attacked about who they are, what they believe, or their morals.

Imagine you're gathering with friends or family, and the conversation turns to an issue you're passionate about. It could be about how people should treat each other, what fairness means, or who's the greatest football player ever.

Everyone has their perspective, but when someone goes against your core beliefs — the fundamental ideas you hold dear — it can feel like a personal attack, even if they didn't mean it that way.

It's like giving your all to build a fantastic sandcastle, and someone says, "That looks terrible." Ouch, right? Your core values and beliefs are like your sandcastle, something you're proud of and hold dear. It's instinctive to defend them when they seem threatened.

This kind of situation has the potential to evoke intense emotions that may cause defensive anger. Our hearts say, "Hey, this is important to me, and I've got to protect it!" It's not just about being right or wrong but feeling respected and understood.

So, how do we handle this better?

- *Pause before you react.*

When you feel the impulse to "defend the castle," take a moment to breathe deeply. Use this pause to collect your thoughts and choose the best response.

- *Express, don't attack.*

Explain why this belief or value matters to you. Using "I feel" statements like "I feel strongly about this because..." can transform the conversation from potentially combative to encouraging mutual understanding and shared perspectives.

- *Agree to disagree.*

  Sometimes, no discussion can change people's minds, and that's okay. It's like having different opinions on pineapple as a pizza topping. Agreeing to disagree means respecting each other's values and staying friendly.

- *Listen to understand.*

  Understanding why someone believes what they do can be eye-opening, even if you disagree. There is no need to alter your opinion; just acknowledge different perspectives.

- *Know when to step back.*

  If the conversation takes a turn for the worse, shifting the focus to another topic is a good idea. Taking care of your inner peace is essential.

  It's natural to want to protect what's important to us, but how we go about it matters. Empathy and respect can improve conversations and strengthen our relationships even when we don't see eye to eye. Next time you feel attacked, try these strategies to avoid getting defensive.

  Identifying these triggers requires self-reflection and honesty. Understanding what usually makes you angry can help you change your reaction. Handling this involves avoiding triggers if you can, mentally preparing for triggers you can't avoid, using coping techniques like deep breathing and mindfulness, or reaching out for support when necessary.

  Understanding triggers isn't about pointing fingers at external factors; it's about taking responsibility for our emotional reactions. Spotting and handling these triggers help us respond better to difficult situations, leading to healthier emotional well-being.

Exercises for recognizing triggers

Here are some simple strategies to help you understand and control your anger:

1. *Keep an interactive anger journal*

Think of yourself as a detective, uncovering the secrets of your emotions. Using an interactive journal can transform the way you handle anger. Whenever you feel your temper flare, grab your journal and jot down the specifics: What triggered it? Who was involved? What actions did you take? How did you feel before and after the incident? This isn't just about venting — it's about getting to the heart of what triggers your anger. As you fill out your journal, treat it like a conversation with a good friend. Over time, you'll notice patterns, such as increased irritability during stressful work or certain people who trigger you. Paying attention to these behaviors is like collecting clues to understand what truly causes your anger.

2. *The HALT technique*

HALT stands for Hungry, Angry, Lonely, and Tired. It's like a quick self-check for when you feel your impatience rising. Are you hungry? Are you upset about something? Or maybe you feel isolated (that's the lonely part) and need to connect. Tiredness can also make things seem worse. Asking yourself these questions helps you prioritize your basic needs, which can be beneficial for relaxing and preventing them from impacting your reactions.

3. *Sensory focus technique*

This approach involves choosing one sense to concentrate on daily — sight, sound, smell, touch, or taste. As you go about your day, pay close attention to what stimulates that sense. For instance, if focusing on hearing, pay attention to the different tones in people's voices, the background noises, and how loud the conversations are. See how these sounds might make you feel, especially if they get on your nerves or anger you. Take a deep breath (or more!) and give yourself a moment to think. What is making you angry? Over time, by reviewing your notes, you will begin to recognize patterns that expose specific triggers. Practicing this regularly will help you become more aware and in control of your reactions, making it easier to manage your anger.

I often say this, but it bears repeating: the goal of these exercises is not to eliminate anger from our lives — an unrealistic and unhelpful goal since anger serves as an important signal. Understanding our anger involves being aware of its presence, acknowledging it when it arises, and consciously choosing responses that promote positive outcomes for ourselves and our relationships. When practiced regularly, these strategies can effectively regulate our emotions and enable us to remain composed, calm, and in charge, regardless of the circumstances.

Self-reflective questions about triggers

Now that we've finished Chapter 2 and explored the different phases of anger and what can set it off, pause to reflect on your struggles with anger. Use these questions to guide you:

1. *Identify triggers*: What situations or behaviors typically trigger your anger? Try to be as specific as possible.

2. *Your physical signs*: Can you identify some physical signs that occur before you start feeling angry? Clenched fists, an accelerated heart rate, or tension in certain body parts?

3. *Understand your needs*: Anger can sometimes cover up our deeper needs or desires. Think about a recent time when you were angry and ask yourself, "What did I really need in that situation?" Maybe it was respect, understanding, some space, or something else entirely.

4. *Evaluate your response*: Consider the last time you were angry. What was your reaction, and how did it influence the situation and the people involved?

5. *The role of HALT*: Reflect on times when hunger, loneliness, fatigue, or other basic needs influenced your impatience. Do you see any patterns in how these needs make your emotions worse?

6. *Techniques for coping*: How have you dealt with your anger before? Which strategies have worked and which haven't? Why?

7. *Seek support*: How easy is it for you to seek support when you're angry? Who do you trust enough to share your feelings with? What makes it easier or harder to reach out to someone?

8. *Set goals*: Reflect on your thoughts and choose one or two specific goals to improve anger management. How will you monitor your progress?

These questions help you understand what makes you angry, explore why you feel this way, and find better ways to handle your anger. Don't worry; we'll explore these topics in the upcoming chapters.

 You can use the workbook to discover your triggers and dive deeper into understanding your anger.

Just scan the code, and you'll get it!

Looking ahead

Moving from recognizing our simmering anger to learning how to relax, we're about to begin an exciting new chapter on Anger as the Emotional Armor. This part focuses on understanding how anger can shield us from deeper emotions we may be unprepared to confront.

Master these tips and tricks, embrace the insights, and prepare for an epic journey of self-discovery and emotional growth.

THE UNBRIDLED STORM

3. Anger, the Emotional Armor

Think of anger as a formidable suit of armor. We often associate rage with being wild and untamed, like a storm that sweeps in and turns everything upside down. But in this chapter, we'll look at anger from a different perspective: as something that, believe it or not, is trying to protect our softer, more sensitive feelings that are hidden inside.

Beneath our anger, we often find feelings like sadness, fear, or disappointment. These emotions can make us feel vulnerable, which can be scary, so we usually respond with rage. Vulnerability can sometimes lead to anger as a defense mechanism for our emotional defenselessness.

In the workbook, you will see a detailed graphic illustrating how this symbolic armor is composed of various layers, each representing a distinct emotional state that adds to the overall experience of anger.

When you're covered in heavy metal from head to toe, it's challenging to feel the sun's warmth on your skin or the gentle touch of a breeze, isn't it?

As we become more aware of our anger and what triggers it, we can slowly remove our protective shield.

The key is to find a balance between holding on and letting go, knowing when to use our armor and when to enjoy the present moment without it.

Anger is your shield

When you feel attacked, criticized, or hurt, anger can create a defense between you and those who cause you pain. This instinctive reaction is a survival mechanism that safeguards our psychological health. While anger can offer temporary protection, it also builds walls that hinder genuine connection and understanding.

If you ever feel like someone is targeting you with metaphorical arrows, such as hurtful words, hostile stares, or a sense of exclusion, consider donning your armor. "Not today," your inner knight proclaims, slipping on the anger armor to guard against the sting of unpleasant feelings. But here's the thing about wearing armor all the time: it gets heavy, and it's hard to give a hug or even a high five when you're rattling around with metal.

While anger can serve as a helpful defense

mechanism, relying on it constantly can isolate you behind impenetrable emotional walls. With this protective barrier, you miss the warmth of friendships and the chance to understand others better.

How can you find a balance between protection and not building a defense?

- *Check in with your armor.*

From time to time, ask yourself, "Do I really need my armor right now? Or is it safe to take it off?" Sometimes, we put it on out of habit, even when there's no battle to fight.

- *Open the drawbridge.*

Find safe ways to let your guard down. You could talk to someone you trust about your feelings or let others know what you need.

- *Remember, it's okay to feel.*

Feeling anger or hurt is a normal part of being human; it's important to remember that you have emotions, too, and you don't always have to be the hero. When we own our feelings without getting defensive, we connect with ourselves.

- *Practice taking off the armor.*

Take it easy at first. Maybe start by not getting upset over small things, like someone being late. See how responding with understanding instead of anger makes you feel.

Knowing when to protect yourself and when to let your guard down keeps you safe and helps build relationships. So, occasionally, take off your armor and enjoy the lighter, more comfortable feeling of being yourself and open to the world.

Your vulnerability, the source of strength

Vulnerability is when we allow ourselves to be seen, truly and completely, scars and all, with the chance of not being accepted. It's about sharing our true thoughts, feelings, and desires, even when we're scared of how the other person might respond. Confronting the hidden emotions beneath our armored shell — the fear that grips our hearts, the shame that weighs us down, the sadness that lingers, and the disappointment that haunts us — takes extraordinary courage.

Embracing and facing these emotions is difficult, but it's where healing starts.

Imagine having an invisible armor suit that keeps you safe from fear, sadness, hurt, and disappointment. This defense provides safety by shielding you from harm. But here's a secret: when you're brave enough to let your guard down and say, "I'm actually feeling scared or sad right now," something amazing happens. It brings to light a secret garden where challenging emotions thrive, waiting to be understood.

Revealing your unprotected inner self can be terrifying. It's like showing someone your favorite, slightly embarrassing dance moves; you do not know how they will react. But expressing your emotions can be a tremendous relief, like dancing without inhibitions. This empowerment is in having the courage to address what truly bothers you, such as feeling excluded or grappling with old wounds that haven't healed. Find out your inner source of fear by doing the exercise in the workbook.

The fantastic thing is that expressing your emotions begins a powerful healing process, like putting a bandage on a scrape instead of pretending it doesn't exist. Being vulnerable not only helps you heal but also allows you to strengthen connections with others. When you share your true selves, imperfections, and all, you encourage others to do the same and foster deeper understanding.

How do you even begin to embrace vulnerability?

- *Take baby steps.*

Start with the little things. Share your genuine reaction to a movie with a friend, or express your fears about an upcoming event.

- *You need safe spaces.*

Find places and people where you can be your true self without worrying. These are the places where you can let your guard down.

- *Listen to yourself.*

Be aware of the messages your emotions are sending you. It's like being your best friend, paying close attention to your needs.

- *It's okay to feel.*

It's completely healthy to experience a range of emotions, even the ones that aren't particularly pleasant, as they add depth to the complex nature of your being.

Embracing vulnerability allows you to release anger and build authentic connections rooted in emotional transparency and understanding. So, take a moment to breathe deeply, express yourself through your unique dance moves, and celebrate the beautiful freedom of being vulnerable as you fully accept your authentic self.

Connecting with your vulnerable side

Imagine that your emotions are like a roiling sea. On the surface, we see the great, crashing waves of anger roaring and echoing through the room. Hidden beneath the waves are vast depths filled with secret treasures and treacherous traps. These emotions make you vulnerable: fear, sadness, shame, inadequacy, and insecurity. Ignoring or repressing them will build up until they explode as massive bursts of rage.

So, how can you dive below the surface in a kind, gentle way? Try these fun exercises.

1. The vulnerability vlog

Start a private video log (vlog) in which you talk about your day, focusing on moments when you felt vulnerable. Describe the situation, how you felt, and why you think you felt that way. Talking to a camera can sometimes feel less intimidating than writing or talking to someone else. Just keep it simple, like you're chatting on a video call with your best friend (You). This approach offers a safe and personalized way to explore and understand your vulnerabilities. It also helps you see your comfort level when sharing your feelings and supports you in improving.

2. The comfort zone challenge

Make it a monthly goal to take small, manageable risks that push you out of your comfort zone. It could involve trying out a new activity, starting a conversation with someone you don't know, or sharing a controversial opinion in a group. Pushing your boundaries in controlled situations can make you more comfortable with vulnerability, increasing resilience and self-confidence.

3. The empathy bond

Share stories of when you felt vulnerable with a friend or family member. Express empathy by taking turns to listen and share without fixing anything or offering advice. It's simply listening and being there for each other. This exercise isn't just about storytelling; it's a powerful way to build trust and deepen connections. Knowing you're not alone in those moments can make all the difference. It's incredibly comforting to discover that we all experience vulnerability.

4. The two sides of the story game

Set up two chairs across from each other. Take a seat and explain why you're upset as if you were talking directly to the person or situation that upset you. Now, switch to the other chair and look at the problem differently. The simple act of changing seats can have a profound impact on your mindset, fostering empathy and understanding.

Practical insight: Try using this technique with someone you trust, like a friend or family member. It can help you gain more understanding and practice resolving conflict through conversation.

5. The vulnerability box

One simple yet powerful way to embrace vulnerability is to create a box with your vulnerabilities. Whenever you notice yourself feeling insecure, unworthy, or afraid, write the vulnerable emotion on a piece of paper and place it in the box. By labeling and containing the feeling, you're acknowledging its presence and setting it aside for now. You can plan to address it more constructively in the future. It's a practice that helps you process emotions and encourages you to approach vulnerability openly when ready.

Set aside time for regular "vulnerability box" reviews to make this ritual more powerful. Sit down and open the box every week, taking one note at a time. Some vulnerabilities may be superficial and no longer need to be addressed; therefore, they can be ignored. Others may require loving self-reflection, journaling, or sharing with a trusted friend. This practice gently guides you through healing insecurities and releasing pent-up emotions. Let's look at Dan's story to better understand the difference.

Dan loved to draw from a young age and often filled his notebooks with colorful sketches. One day, during a class art project, his teacher made a careless remark, criticizing his work as "messy" and "unimaginative." This comment struck deeply, making Dan feel embarrassed and ashamed of his artistic abilities.

From that moment, Dan became fearful of showcasing his art. He stopped drawing altogether, fearing further criticism and rejection. This early experience planted a seed of self-doubt, causing him to hide his talents and avoid situations where his work might be judged. Dan's fear persisted as an adult, preventing him from exploring and enjoying his creative potential. Now, let's analyze and identify the difference.

Superficial vulnerability: Sharing artwork

Although it may seem significant, Dan's reluctance to show his work is a surface vulnerability. He overcame it by sharing his art with his loved ones to conquer fear. The encouraging comments and acts of showcasing boosted his confidence. He discovered that the joy of creating and expressing himself was far more important than the fear of being judged. This helped him break free from his vulnerability, realizing it was no longer necessary to focus on.

Deeper vulnerability: Fear of not being good enough

The real issue lies in Dan's persistent fear of not being good enough, which stems from his early discouragement. This seemingly one-time critique has had a negative echo on his confidence in various areas of his life, including art, relationships, career, and self-worth. Once he realized how deeply ingrained this insecurity was, through therapy, he could trace its roots and understand how it influenced his decisions and self-image. Healing from this vulnerability requires self-love, patience, and continuous support.

A quick note here: please seek professional help when you feel overwhelmed.

6. The emotions playlist

Music has a unique power to touch our emotions. If you're dealing with anger (or any other overwhelming emotion), listen to a song that reflects your current state.

Choose a happier song to boost your mood when you start feeling better. Organize your playlist by emotion and include notes about what each song means to you. This adds a personal touch to the experience and enhances music's effectiveness as an emotional exploration tool.

Your emotional well-being greatly depends on your capacity to recognize and explore your feelings. As a psychologist, I often recommend exercises my clients can easily do at home. So don't be afraid to start with any of these exercises. Use the workbook to personalize your journey.

Discover your inner armor

This third chapter examined how anger acts as a shield for your most delicate feelings. As you peel back the layers of your anger, it's important to take a moment to understand the insights you've gained about yourself and your emotional responses. Use these questions to guide you:

1. *What's behind your shield*: Think about a recent experience of anger. Do you know the more profound emotion causing you to hide behind anger? What difference did it make to acknowledge that emotion in your answer?

2. *The weight of your armor*: How has being angry all the time affected your interactions with others? Can you think of a situation where anger made things more complicated than needed?

3. *Cracks in your armor:* Have there been moments when your anger couldn't shield you completely, making you feel exposed or even more vulnerable? What happened?

4. *Put down your shield:* Recall a time when you didn't react angrily and instead focused on the underlying emotion. What was the result, and how did you feel?

5. *The cost of your protection:* In what ways has using anger as a defense mechanism cost you opportunities for deeper connection or personal growth? Consider what you may have missed.

6. *Find new tools:* What strategies have you learned in this chapter to replace anger as a means of self-protection? How can you use these strategies in your daily life?

7. *The strength of vulnerability:* Think about when being open and vulnerable led to something positive. How did expressing your true feelings instead of staying angry improve the situation or relationship?

8. *The path forward:* What can you do to continue understanding the emotions behind your anger? How can you remind yourself to pause and reflect instead of reacting angrily to similar situations in the future?

9. *The vision of growth:* Picture yourself one year from now, using the knowledge and strategies from this chapter. In what ways have you changed your approach to anger and vulnerability?

Looking ahead

Just think of your anger as a volcano inside you, starting quietly but getting louder and harder to ignore. In the upcoming section of our journey, we will concentrate on identifying and managing this brewing volcano before it erupts into a massive explosion.

We'll continue to discuss ways to identify early warnings, acknowledge their presence, and, most importantly, stop them before they become major trouble.

 Take a moment and go to the workbook to practice expressing your emotions openly, even the ones that scare you or make you feel defenseless. Learn how to allow yourself to be a little vulnerable. To get the workbook just scan the code if you haven't done so already.

NAVIGATING THE STORM

4. Roaring Winds Ahead

Let me tell you about Theo, a small-town baker known for his delicious pastries and friendly smile. But Theo had a secret that few people knew about: he was angry, building up like a pot about to boil over.

He was so passionate and absorbed in his business that he didn't even realize how stressed he was getting. He just kept on going, totally focused on his work. But the air conditioning broke down one boiling summer afternoon during the town's annual fair. It was too hot to stand, and dealing with long lines and special orders made things even worse. Theo could feel the stress building, and his patience was running out like the frosting on his cinnamon rolls.

The last straw was when a novice dropped a big order of pastries for the main event of the fair, making the treats useless. His normally repressed anger erupted in a torrent of harsh words and rebukes, leaving the employee in tears and the bakery in stunned silence. The sudden outburst of temper had damaged his relationship with his employees, customers, and his small business's reputation. Afterward, Theo understood that his anger was a ticking time bomb, ready to explode and destroy the foundation of his life's work and relationships.

Determined to defuse the bomb, he realized he needed to find effective ways to calm down. This journey led him to research methods and actively seek answers rather than letting his anger build up. Therapy helped Theo discover what made him angry. He understood that, besides the stress of running a bakery, his anger was also a result of his fear of failing and not meeting his standards.

Can you relate to Theo's story? Have you ever felt like a balloon that keeps getting blown up but is about to burst? This vivid image shows how we feel when our anger is out of control. It builds up slowly, ticking away, until suddenly it explodes, shattering our peace.

This chapter focuses on identifying early signs of anger, mastering strategies to calm it down, and staying safe from its effects. Let's see some practical techniques I use for keeping calm and managing anger when things get heated.

Simple anger management strategies

First and foremost, we need to recognize the importance of anger management. It's like hearing a smoke alarm go off and taking it seriously. Letting our anger take over can negatively affect our relationships, jobs, and feelings about ourselves. Understanding that anger isn't just something to shrug off but a signal that needs immediate attention is key to personal harmony.

Next, we will look at specific, actionable strategies for stopping the anger in its tracks. We will start with the two easiest-to-use and simplest reflection exercises that my clients often use.

1. The 10 things count

This technique helps to shift your attention and refocus your mind, which can be useful when dealing with anger. When you start to feel irritated, take a moment to pause and then shift your attention to counting ten things around you. These can be things you can touch, hear, or see different colors nearby. This is how you can practice it:

- The first step is to *become aware of your emotional state* and acknowledge your annoyance.
- *Take a breath.*

Once you realize you're getting irritated, stop what you're doing and take a deep breath to help calm your initial emotional surge. Breathing deeply helps slow down the physiological arousal that anger can bring.

- *Begin to count.*

Look around and start counting ten different things you can see. For example, you might notice a book, a plant, a cup, a picture on the wall, a light switch, and so forth. Engage your mind in a simple task that requires a bit of focus but isn't too demanding.

- *Include other senses.*

If you're in a place where you can't easily find ten things to count, or if you find the visual task too easy, try engaging your other senses: sounds you can hear, things you can touch, smell, or taste.

- *Reflect.*

After you've counted to ten, take a moment to assess your emotional state. Has your annoyance lessened? Do you feel more in control? This observation can help you understand the connection between the distraction and its impact on your anger.

Why does it work?

- *Anger can tunnel our attention towards provoking stimuli or thoughts.*

Counting different things distracts your mind from the source of anger, giving your emotions time to subside and your rational mind a chance to catch up.

- *This technique encourages you to notice details in your immediate environment*, grounding you in the present moment and away from the spiraling thoughts that anger can provoke.
- Counting to ten *serves as a cognitive interruption*, breaking the cycle of escalating anger and preventing the emotional response from overwhelming.

Here's how to take it to the next level:

- *Mix up the categories.*

Instead of simply naming what you can see, try identifying what you can hear, smell, or touch. This will engage different brain parts and distract you from your anger.

- *Make it a game.*

Challenge yourself to find ten objects of a specific color or ten distinct sounds. This adds playfulness to the distraction technique.

Feel free to adapt the counting to suit your preferences or the situation's specifics. Some people find counting backward or specific colors or object types helpful. I encourage my clients to work on this technique when they're feeling relaxed so it will come more naturally to them when they're under stress. I encourage you, too!

2. The water trick

In anger management, the "water trick" is a straightforward yet highly effective technique for calming the body's response to anger. This method involves using water to cool down both emotionally and physically and hydrate at the same time. It's important to act deliberately when you feel anger starting to rise.

- *Recognize the signs.*

Learn to identify the early signs of anger — maybe your heart races, your breathing speeds up, or you feel tension in your shoulders.

- *Reach for water.*

As soon as you notice these signs, pause and drink a glass of water slowly. Focus on the act of drinking: observe the temperature of the water, the sensation as it flows down your throat, and the sound of the water in the glass.

- *Cooldown.*

If possible, splash some cold water on your face. Cooling down and giving your system a temperature shock can reduce anger's physical sensations.

- *Reflect.*

Use the time you spend drinking water to consider why you're angry. Do you need to do something about it now, or can you deal with it later when you're calmer?

Why does it work?

- *It has a physiological impact.*

Drinking water and splashing cold water on your face can help lower your body temperature, which often rises during anger. This physical cooling can signal your brain to calm down.

- *It interrupts anger response.*

Engaging in a physical activity like drinking water interrupts the escalating process of anger. This break can give you enough time to engage your rational brain, evaluate the situation more clearly, and respond rather than react.

- *It calms the mind, a great mindfulness exercise.*

Focusing on the act of drinking water brings mindfulness into play, forcing you to concentrate on the present and distract yourself from the anger-inducing trigger. Being mindful can make you less reactive and improve how you handle your emotions.

Keep a bottle of water handy at your desk, in your car, or in your bag. Making water easily accessible ensures you can use this technique anytime and anywhere you feel anger rising. Enhance the calming effect by adding a slice of lemon or cucumber to your water or a few drops of calming essential oils like lavender or mint. Experiment with different temperatures. Some people find cold water refreshing and helpful, while others may find warm water soothing.

Next, here are some reflective exercises designed to

deepen your insights into how anger manifests in your life and how to manage it:

1. The anger diary

We've touched on the idea of using an anger diary, but now let me better underline that it's not just about noting when you're feeling angry; it's also a tool for getting to know yourself better. Let's see how to make the most of it:

- *Be specific.*

When describing an episode of anger, be as specific as possible. What exactly was said or done that made you angry? Details are important because they can reveal how sensitive you are on a deeper level.

- *Rate your anger.*

On a scale of 1 to 10, rate how angry you felt. This can help you see if specific triggers consistently lead to stronger reactions. Note any physical sensations you experienced. Did your heart race? Did you feel hot? Recognizing these signs can help you become more aware of your anger in real-time, allowing you to manage it before it escalates.

- *Reflect on the resolution.*

When the situation is resolved, document what happened. Was there anything specific that helped you calm down or resolve the conflict? This may give you ideas for strategies to try in the future.

2. The 5 "why" deep dives

This is my favorite, and I often use it with my clients. Pick a recent episode of anger from your journal. Ask yourself, "Why?" five times to get to the bottom of your anger. For example, "Why did that comment make me angry?" could lead to "Why does feeling ignored bother me so much?" It's like peeling an onion to get to the root of the problem.

Here is how to dig deeper:

- *Start with the surface.*

Begin with the immediate reason you became angry and keep asking, "Why?" Don't stop at the first or second answer; push yourself deeper.

- *Look for patterns.*

As you ask "Why?" you may begin to notice patterns. Perhaps issues of respect, recognition, or fairness keep coming up. These patterns point to your core values and areas where you're particularly sensitive.

- *Consider the context.*

Sometimes, our anger has as much to do with our current state as with the trigger. Were you already stressed out or tired? Understanding the context can help you see that your anger may not be entirely about the immediate situation.

- *Explore alternatives.*

Once you have identified the deeper reasons for your anger, ask yourself how you might react differently. Knowing why something bothers you so much can give you the power to change your response.

If you make these strategies a part of your daily routine, you'll have better control over your anger and avoid doing or saying anything you'll regret later.

Quick and effective anger-busting methods

Calming anger involves more than avoiding outbursts; it's about finding peace and clarity during moments of frustration. I want to share a few highly effective strategies for alleviating anger.

1. The 5-second pause

Pausing is a powerful tool that should not be overlooked. When anger flares, your first impulse may be to react, but those reactions can escalate the situation. This method puts a brief stop between your anger and your actions, allowing you to choose a response rather than react impulsively. Here's a detailed look at how to use the 5-second pause and why it's so effective.

- *Recognize and acknowledge.*

The first step is to recognize that you're feeling angry. Acknowledgment is crucial because you can't address what

you don't accept. Notice the signs of anger building up —
perhaps your heart rate increases, your breathing becomes
rapid, or you feel a heat flush through your body.

- *Pause.*

Once you recognize these signs, immediately pause your
words, step back, and give yourself a moment to just breathe.
Count slowly to five. Each count should be a deliberate
second long, and with each number, focus on drawing in a
deep breath and then exhaling slowly.

- *Assess.*

During the pause, quickly assess the situation. Ask yourself
why you're angry. What triggered your anger? Is your reaction
proportionate to the problem?

- *Choose.*

Decide how best to respond. This moment of pause allows
you to choose a reply that aligns with your best intentions and
reflects a more thoughtful approach rather than a
spontaneous emotional reaction.

Why does it work?

- *Interrupts the anger cycle.*

The 5-second pause helps to disturb the automatic
physiological response to anger. By pausing, you stop the
flood of stress hormones like cortisol and adrenaline,
preventing the situation from escalating.

- *Engages the prefrontal cortex.*

Slowing down and counting to ten involves the part of the brain responsible for decision-making and impulse control. This shift in brain activity helps you move from an emotionally charged state to a more rational state.

- *Creates space for reflection.*

This brief interlude allows you to reflect on the consequences of your potential reactions. It's a moment to consider the outcomes of your actions, helping to prevent regrettable decisions that could damage relationships or lead to other negative consequences.

Some people find it helpful to visualize a stop sign during the pause. This can serve as a visual cue to halt all actions and thoughts.

To reinforce the pause, combine it with a physical action. For example, press your fingertips together, place your hand on your heart, or gently tap your foot on the ground.

2. Deep breathing

It is like a cool breeze on a hot day for your nervous system. As a psychologist, I often emphasize the importance of deep breathing as a response to rising anger and a preventative tool to manage stress and emotional reactivity.

Deep breathing involves taking slow, controlled breaths deep into your lungs, filling them fully, and then exhaling completely. This type of breathing is also known as diaphragmatic, abdominal, or belly. Here's a step-by-step guide on how to practice it:

- *Find a comfortable position.*

Sit in a comfy chair with your back straight, or lie on a flat surface. Place one hand on your chest and the other on your stomach.

- *Breathe in slowly through your nose*, allowing your stomach to rise as much as possible while keeping your chest relatively still.
- *Hold your breath for three to four seconds.*

This pause can help increase your oxygen absorption.

- *Exhale slowly and completely through your mouth.*

As you blow air out, purse your lips slightly, but keep your jaw relaxed. You may use a quiet, whooshing sound as you exhale.

- *Repeat this process for several minutes.*

You can start with one to two minutes and gradually increase the time as you become more comfortable with the practice.

- *You can combine your breathing with a calming phrase or mantra.*

Breathe in "I am" and breathe out "at peace." This can help center your thoughts away from anger.

Why is it effective?

- *Reduces stress hormones.*

Deep breathing helps decrease the production of "stress hormones" such as cortisol and adrenaline. Lowering these hormones can help reduce the physical and emotional intensity of anger.

- *Activates the parasympathetic nervous system.*
This type of breathing triggers the "rest and digest" system which is responsible for calming the body and restoring it to a state of balance.

- *Improves oxygen exchange.*
Deep breathing enhances oxygen and carbon dioxide exchange in your blood. This increased oxygenation can calm your mind and body, helping you think more clearly and reduce feelings of anxiety or anger.

- *Focuses the mind.*
Attention to your breath can distract you from anger triggers, giving you time to gain perspective and react more thoughtfully.

Some people find it helpful to visualize the air flowing in and out or imagine a peaceful scene while practicing deep breathing. This can enhance the relaxation effect. Deep breathing is a versatile tool you can easily adapt to fit into any lifestyle and perform almost anywhere.

3. Change the environment

Changing the environment is a strategic and effective technique that can help mitigate the intensity of your anger. Sometimes, it is best to physically distance yourself from the source of your anger.

Here are some ways to do this effectively:

- *Take a walk*. A quick stroll, especially outdoors, can work wonders. The physical activity helps burn off some of the adrenaline fueling your anger, and the change of scenery can help shift your perspective.
- *Seek out nature*. If possible, find a park or green space. Nature has a calming effect on the mind and can help you reset emotionally.

4. Use humor

Imagine you're stuck in a traffic jam, running late for an important meeting. The cars ahead of you aren't moving, your frustration is boiling over, and all you can think about is how unfair this situation feels. Now, picture a clown walking between the cars, handing out balloons. Ridiculous, right? But isn't there something about the absurdity of this mental image that makes you want to laugh? That tiny giggle might just be enough to shift your perspective, to remind you that not every problem is as dire as it seems.

Here's a personal story. I once worked with a client, let's call him John, who struggled with road rage. His anger would spike whenever he hit a red light or got cut off in traffic. We devised a strategy together where he kept a playlist of his favorite comedy sketches in the car. Every time he felt his anger rising, he would hit play. Over time, he noticed that the humor helped him see the lighter side of these frustrating situations, and his road rage incidents decreased significantly.

The science backs this up, too. Laughter triggers the release of endorphins, our brain's feel-good chemicals, which help reduce stress and improve our overall mood. It also lowers cortisol levels, the stress hormone, which can be elevated during moments of anger.

I emphasize the careful and thoughtful use of humor as a strategy for diffusing anger, not just because it can lighten the mood but because it shifts our perspective, offering a new way of seeing a situation that might otherwise set us off. However, it's crucial to wield this tool wisely, as inappropriate or ill-timed humor can exacerbate tensions rather than ease them.

Here's a deeper look at how humor can help manage anger and some guidelines for using it effectively.

- *Breaks the tension*

Humor offers a way to break the tension that builds up in a heated moment. A well-timed joke or humorous observation can act like a release valve, allowing everyone involved to laugh and reducing anger's physiological intensity. Laughter triggers the release of endorphins, the body's natural feel-good chemicals, which can help calm the nerves and lighten the mood.

- *Promotes bonding*

    Laughing together can bring people closer, even when things are tense. Creating bonds with others can help prevent feelings of isolation and being misunderstood when angry.

- *Provides perspective*

    Humor can make problems feel less overwhelming by giving us a different perspective. It invites us not to take ourselves too seriously and to see the absurdity or the lighter side of whatever is causing the anger. This shift in perspective can often be enough to stop anger from escalating.

    Let's think about a situation where humor can help diffuse anger, which many of us can connect with, like assembling furniture with overly complicated instructions. You're at home, surrounded by panels, screws, and a booklet that seems to have been written in an ancient, cryptic language. The frustration mounts with every passing minute, and you can feel the anger rising, as what should have been a simple chair looks more like a modern art sculpture gone wrong. Now, pause and imagine you're in a sitcom.

    The audience is out there, laughing not at you but with you about the absurdity of the situation. You start narrating your actions out loud, like a DIY show host with no idea what they're doing. "*And here we have the rare and elusive 'flange sprocket,' crucial for the stability of... absolutely nothing.*" You look at the camera that isn't there and shrugs, "*Who needs four legs on a chair, anyway? Three is the new trend; it adds a bit of excitement to every sit-down.*"

This shift in perspective, treating the frustrating task as a comedy sketch, allows you to laugh at the situation and yourself. A happier mood and perhaps even a sincere chuckle at the situation replace the waning anger. Instead of a battle with inanimate objects, it becomes a memorable, laugh-worthy episode in the sitcom of your life. The chair might still wobble, but your mood has stabilized, all thanks to finding humor in the moment's absurdity.

Here's a guide on using humor wisely and respectfully

- *Tailor your humor* to the people around you and avoid jokes that touch on sensitive subjects or personal issues.
- *Sarcasm can be risky*, especially in tense situations. It can easily be misinterpreted and might come across as mocking or belittling. If you choose to use sarcasm, ensure it is gentle and that your relationship with the other person can withstand this level of teasing.
- *Humor that pokes gentle fun* at yourself can be very effective because it shows that you are open and not taking yourself too seriously, which can encourage others to relax. However, be mindful that too much self-deprecation does not affect your self-esteem.

- *The timing of your humor is crucial.* Introducing humor when someone expresses serious concerns or is highly agitated might not be well received. Wait for a lull in the intensity of the emotion or when the other person seems open to shifting gears.

After attempting humor, *gauge the reaction* of the other person or people involved. Your humor is likely well-received if they respond positively and seem to relax. If not, be prepared to shift tactics, perhaps offering a sincere apology.

5. Express your feelings in a non-threatening language.

Aside from my clients, I often use it with my loved ones. With "I" statements, you can communicate your feelings and help prevent many conflicts from escalating. Of course, we will do more examples in the workbook, but for now, here are some tips for using them:

- *Be specific about your feelings.*

Instead of saying, "I'm angry," identify the underlying feeling. "I feel ignored" or "I feel stressed" may be more meaningful.

- *Focus on the behavior, not the person.*

"I get frustrated when meetings start late" is more constructive than blaming someone for always being late.

- *Express your needs clearly.*

After voicing your feelings, follow up with a straightforward request. "I need us to start on time so that I can manage my workload effectively."

Instead of suppressing your anger, try using these techniques to express it in a way that fosters understanding and respect.

Thought-provoking questions

The self-reflection questions are based on Chapter 4, where we learn about recognizing and managing anger before it becomes uncontrollable, and also include some insights we've already covered:

1. Reflect on the last time you lost your temper. What was the trigger? Think about the emotions and thoughts that happened earlier.

2. What happened after you lost your temper? How did it affect your relationships, your self-esteem, or your day?

3. When you get angry, what changes do you notice in your body or mind?

4. Can you think of a time when pausing before responding could have made a difference?

5. Think back to a time when deep breaths helped you relax. What changes did it make in your body and mind? If

you haven't already used it, what's stopping you?

6. Think of a time when changing your environment (going for a walk or moving to another room) could have helped to diffuse your anger. How do you think it could have made a difference? If you didn't try this, are you going to?

7. Have you ever used humor to calm down when angry or stressed? What impact did it have? Did anyone ever misinterpret your joke?

8. Reflect on a past argument and imagine how using "I" statements could have allowed you to express your emotions without worsening the situation. When you're upset, are you comfortable using "I" statements to express yourself?

9. From experiences where anger played a role, what have you learned about your needs, boundaries, or triggers? How will this information help you manage your anger better in the future?

Take your time and be honest with your answers. They will remind you about some breakthroughs you've had so far so you can use them better. Remember distinct moments when you felt angry, as this will help you understand what triggers your anger, recognize warning signs, and choose your answer.

 Then, go to the workbook, see how anger feels in your body, choose and practice techniques to calm your temper.

Looking ahead

In the next chapter, "Steering Through the Tempest," I will share more insights and strategies about the emotional impact of anger and how we can find clarity in these moments. We will talk about mind detox and the art of understanding.

5. Steering Through the Tempest

When we experience anger, our bodies and minds trigger a chain reaction, a natural response to safeguard us from potential danger.

Anger can be likened to a dense fog that blankets our thoughts, hindering our ability to think clearly and make rational choices. This emotional state signals our body, releasing hormones like adrenaline and cortisol, readying us for fight or flight.

Such physiological changes heighten our senses and narrow our attention, further disorienting us in the heat of the moment.

Emotional impact of anger

Have you ever noticed how anger can alter our perception, amplify issues, and cloud our understanding of situations? When you're angry, your mind often rushes to conclusions, imagines threats that aren't real, and interprets neutral actions as hostile. This skewed view dramatically impacts how you interact and make choices.

We'll discuss further how anger changes how we see things and share tips for clearing our minds of this fog.

1. *Jumping to conclusions*

Engulfed in anger, our minds fixate on perceived injustices or slights, causing us to "jump to conclusions" without considering all the facts or other points of view.

Think about this situation we've all experienced. You text a friend about your exciting upcoming plans, eagerly waiting for a reply that never comes. Your instinctive reaction? You feel frustrated, and your mind starts racing. "*Is she/he ignoring me*?" "*Did I do something wrong*?" This is a typical example of anger clouding our judgment and making us jump to conclusions.

In moments of anger, our brains have difficulty seeing the bigger picture. They act like overzealous detectives assembling a puzzle with missing pieces, often preparing for the worst. When a text goes unanswered, your brain might jump to the conclusion that your friend is choosing to ignore you. Why? Anger makes us so stubborn that we can't think about other options.

Let's briefly clear the fog and explore other reasons your friend may not respond. Maybe they're overwhelmed with work and haven't checked their phone; maybe their battery is dying; or perhaps they're dealing with a personal issue and don't feel up to text. Countless reasons don't involve you. Have you ever ignored a text before? It happens to all of us. The text gets a reply at the end, but maybe not right when we want it.

To prevent unnecessary stress, I'll share strategies to help you break through anger's fog and avoid impulsive reactions.

- *Pause for perspective.*

Before you let anger take over, take a deep breath. Remind yourself that there are many reasons for a delayed reaction, most of which are not personal.

- *Give the benefit of the doubt.*

Practice assuming the best rather than the worst. Your friend may be having a difficult day and will get back to you when they can.

- *Communicate openly.*

If the lack of response bothers you, calmly express your feelings. A simple message like, "Hey, I was worried when I didn't hear from you. Is everything okay?" can promote understanding without making any accusations or assumptions.

- *Reflect on past experiences.*

Think of a time when you could not immediately respond to a message. Were you intentionally ignoring your friend, or were there other reasons for your behavior? Thinking about our experiences helps us relate to others and not be all impulsive.

If we acknowledge how swiftly anger causes us to make hasty assumptions and actively seek to eliminate confusion, we can reduce a significant amount of stress in our lives and relationships. It means giving our minds time to process the information before our feelings overwhelm us.

2. Seeing a threat where there is none

Anger triggers a physiological response known as the fight-or-flight state, which can cause us to interpret harmless situations as threatening due to heightened sensitivity. It's like we've flipped a switch and turned on this state.

While this primal survival instinct is effective in life-or-death situations, such as evading a saber-toothed tiger, it proves less beneficial in today's world, where perceived threats can be as harmless as a text message or a casual remark from a colleague about the workload. The increased vigilance is supposed to keep us safe but sometimes leads to seeing enemies where there aren't any.

Imagine a situation that happens often. You're at work, and a coworker says, "Wow, we're swamped right now, aren't we?" Innocent enough, right? But if you're already nervous or under pressure, your fight-or-flight system may interpret this as a criticism of your ability to keep up or even a sign that you're not doing your part. Suddenly, what should be a sympathetic comment about the workload feels like a personal attack.

This misunderstanding can cause people to become defensive and create tension. You could respond with anger, silence, or resentment, believing you're defending yourself against an imaginary threat. Your colleague is confused and doesn't understand why a small comment about workload upset you.

Situations like this highlight how anger and our automatic response can alter our perceptions. Here's what you can do to stop it from happening:

- *Identify the trigger.*

The first thing to do is understand that anger can mess with your perception of threats. If you acknowledge this, you can pause for a moment and think about what's going on.

- *Question your interpretation.*

When someone's words or actions make you feel threatened, ask yourself, "Is there another way to interpret this? Could I be reading more into this than what's there?"

Instead of reacting defensively, seek clarification. Asking, "Can you tell me more about what you mean?" often reveals that the perceived threat wasn't real.

Understanding how the body reacts to anger and skews the perception of threat allows us to manage the response more effectively. With this awareness, we can handle daily encounters with people more smoothly and without unnecessary drama. This small change brings more peace and happiness to our lives and work.

3. Labeling neutral actions as hostile

Anger acts like a pair of glasses, tinting everything darker than reality. It creates a perception of a hostile world and makes people's actions seem more menacing. Anger affects not only our mood but also our perspective on the world. Our brain activates a defensive mechanism to safeguard us from perceived dangers. But what if those dangers only exist in our thoughts?

Think of a typical scenario where a coworker emails you about the project's status. The email is simple, straightforward, and neutral. But if you're already super mad, maybe from a crappy day or a ton of work, that anger might make you read the email all wrong.

You might take it as a criticism of how fast or dedicated you are instead of just a request. This misunderstanding is based on an illusion of criticism that doesn't exist. "Why are they questioning me? Do they think I'm slacking?" A seemingly innocent request for information unexpectedly turns into an attack.

This twisted perspective has the potential to create significant conflict. You might get defensive and curtly respond or ask what your colleague did for the project. Your coworker who wants an update might feel defensive, resulting in shock or anger because of miscommunication. This is how anger can turn a regular email into a perceived attack, setting off a never-ending cycle of misunderstanding and resentment over what was just a tiny mix-up.

How do you clear the lens?

- *Pause before you interpret.*

When you feel a surge of anger or defensiveness over something minor, give yourself a moment to take a deep breath, acknowledge your initial reaction, and refrain from acting immediately.

- *Clarify any ambiguous messages or actions* to avoid jumping to negative conclusions.

Simply asking, "Can you explain?" you can uncover the true intent and resolve anger-fueled misunderstandings.

- *Check your filters.*

Acknowledge that your current emotional state may color your perceptions. Understanding this emotional filter can help you discern whether your interpretations are rooted in facts or feelings.

- *Practice empathy.*

Put yourself in the other person's shoes and try to understand their perspective. How would you prefer your message to be understood if the situation were reversed? This approach can prevent anger and make it easier to have a constructive discussion.

- *Reflect on past misunderstandings.*

Think about times when anger made you misunderstand a situation. What was the result? Taking time to reflect on these moments can help you notice patterns and make better decisions in the future.

So now you see how anger can mess up your perception, making you think even innocent stuff is a threat. Try to be more mindful of your responses and cultivate healthier, more positive relationships with others. In our daily lives, this fog of anger can hinder good decision-making and aggravate conflicts.

Mind detox

I'm about to share practical techniques from my experience as a psychologist that will help you recalibrate, clear your mind, and see situations more objectively. Here they are:

1. The STOP technique

This technique is like hitting the pause button on your emotions. Here's how it breaks down:

- *Stop. Literally, just stop.*

Freeze for a moment. This holds the anger in its tracks before it takes over completely.

- *Take a deep breath through your nose*, hold it for a few seconds, and then slowly exhale through your mouth.

This simple action can alleviate anger symptoms and bring peace to your mind.

- *Observe.*

Notice what you're thinking and feeling. What's making you angry? Try to name your feelings and thoughts. For example, "I'm upset because I think my work is being unfairly criticized."

- Now that you've cooled down and assessed your feelings, *decide* how you want to respond.

You may choose to address the issue calmly or decide it's not worth your energy right now.

2. Take perspective

Seeing things from the other person's perspective is like flipping a switch and bringing light to a dark room. It sheds light on things you couldn't see before.

- *Ask questions.*

If you're unsure about someone's actions, ask them politely for an explanation. It could be as simple as "I noticed you seemed a little short with me earlier. Is everything okay?"

- *Imagine their side.*

Try to put yourself in their shoes. What challenges are they going through? What were their intentions? It can shift your mindset from opposition to empathy.

Keep in mind that everyone goes through tough times. **Sometimes, when someone seems to attack you, it's their way of dealing with their problems.** I understand it's not easy to accept, but it's true. These moments require patience more than ever.

3. Fact check

Our minds are great at creating stories, especially when feeling emotional. However, not all stories are real. Fact-checking helps you separate the real from the unreal.

- *List the facts.*

Write a description of what happened, sticking to the facts. Seeing it in writing can bring clarity.

- *Question your interpretation.*

Consider each assumption and ask yourself, "Do I have solid evidence for this?" If you answer no, it might be worth reconsidering your stance.

- *Seek clarification.*

When in doubt, seek information directly from the source. Misunderstandings frequently lead to anger, but a simple conversation can help clarify things. Ask open-ended questions and try not to make assumptions before hearing the answers. Using "I" statements is the best way to open up communication.

These few techniques yield remarkable results. Each solution in this book is tailored to the particular anger challenge discussed in that chapter. Therefore, I strongly encourage you to use them. They will enable you to de-escalate anger and make decisions that benefit everyone involved. Instead of trying to avoid anger, manage it effectively and improve your well-being and relationships.

That's our goal here!

The art of understanding

Miscommunication can cause conflict when people misunderstand and make assumptions. For example, during a team meeting, you might suggest an idea that could improve efficiency. However, you phrase it as, "*Maybe we could try doing it this way,*" intending to sound open and collaborative. One of your team members interprets your suggestion as uncertainty about the current process and a lack of confidence in your idea. They respond defensively, emphasizing the reasons why the current method works well while seemingly dismissing your suggestion out of hand.

The misunderstanding happened because your attempt to be collaborative came across as hesitant, which led to a defensive response and a missed chance for productive conversation.

This discord causes a conflict where you feel unheard, and your teammate seems resistant to change because the meaning of your words gets lost in translation. You should work on your communication skills to prevent this from happening again.

Let me share some practical tips to improve your communication skills and make conflict resolution a breeze.

1. Active listening

This kind of listening goes beyond waiting for your chance to speak. It involves being genuinely interested in what the other person has to say.

- *Maintain gentle eye contact* to show that you're focused and engaged.
- *Lean forward slightly or nod occasionally* to show interest and that you listen.
- *Paraphrase what you've heard* to confirm understanding, such as, "So what I'm hearing is that you feel overwhelmed by the workload, right?"

- *Encourage them to share* by asking, "Tell me more about how that made you feel?"

2. "I" statements

When you use "I" statements, conversations can become more open and honest instead of defensive.
Here's the framing technique:

- *Express emotion*: Begin by saying, "I feel..."
- *Briefly describe the situation without placing blame.* "...when meetings go overtime..."
- *Explain the impact.* Share how the situation affects you. "...because it makes it difficult for me to manage my workload."
- *Avoid "you" accusations*: Saying "you always" or "you never" can make the other person feel attacked and can cause them to shut down and not say anything.

3. Assertive communication

It can be challenging to find the right balance between advocating for yourself and considering the needs of others. Clear and respectful communication of thoughts, feelings, and needs, along with mindful consideration of others' rights and boundaries, is essential.

Assertiveness is key to effectively managing anger and keeping relationships healthy. Finding the right balance between standing up for yourself and being considerate of others takes practice.

Here's how you can do it:

- *Clearly state what you need* or what is concerning you. Cut to the chase and avoid unnecessary rambling.
- *Make sure to keep your language polite* and avoid insults or attempts to belittle others.
- *Use "we" whenever possible.* It underscores the value of togetherness. "Let's figure out a solution together?"

It's natural to feel uncomfortable when starting to be assertive, especially if you're used to being passive or aggressive. Build your confidence by practicing with minor issues.

4. Seek solutions.

Focusing on finding solutions instead of dwelling on problems promotes teamwork and helps us learn and grow from conflicts. Here's the approach:

- *Encourage the other person to join you in brainstorming solutions*. It gives them a sense of being included and valued.
- *Be open to compromise.* Sometimes, the best solution involves a little give-and-take from both sides.
- *Create an action plan*. After agreeing on a solution, create a plan and the steps needed to make it happen. This shows a firm commitment to resolving the issue.

- *Make it a habit to check in regularly* and evaluate the solution's progress. This shows that we care and are willing to make changes when necessary.

These communication skills will help you connect with others, avoid discord, complete tasks faster, and build healthy relationships.

Your communication style

After reading Chapter 5, "Steering Through the Tempest," and learning about how anger affects our judgment and leads to misunderstandings, here are some questions to help you reflect on and enhance your communication skills.

1. Can you remember a time when anger affected your decision-making? Describe how it did.

2. Have you ever jumped to conclusions about someone's actions or words because you were angry? Think about the situation and how it turned out once you had all the facts.

3. Can you think of a time when you saw something that wasn't hostile or dangerous but thought it was? What happened, and how did you determine your view was incorrect?

4. How often do you practice active listening, especially when feeling defensive or angry?

5. Think about a recent conflict where using "I" statements could have changed the flow of the conversation. How could you have expressed your feelings and needs without blaming others?

6. Can you give examples of when you were assertive in your communication? Are there any situations where you find it hard to be assertive? Why do you think this is?

7. Reflect on a conflict that had a positive resolution. How did seeking solutions and problem-solving help find a resolution?

8. What is your usual reaction when someone challenges your opinions or presents a different viewpoint? Do you struggle or find it easy to consider viewpoints other than your own?

9. What can you do to calm down when you're feeling angry or defensive?

10. How can better communication help you avoid misunderstandings and resolve conflicts? Choose one or two communication skills you want to work on.

Before moving on to the next chapter, go to the  workbook and take a moment to personalize your learning on how anger warps your reality and practice effective communication techniques to handle conflicts and clear misunderstandings. Simply scan the code if you haven't done so already.

Looking ahead

Now that we've seen how anger affects us, we know its impact and can do something to prevent getting overwhelmed and making impulsive decisions. It's important to remember that managing anger goes beyond avoiding fights. It's more about building healthy connections with the people in our lives as we learn and grow.

NAVIGATING THE STORM

6. The Heavy Burden

Left unresolved, anger can become a broken record, repeating patterns of frustration, outbursts, and regret. As a psychologist, I've witnessed how these unresolved emotions create repetitive patterns in our lives that affect not only our mental health but also our physical health. Through personal stories, we will explore the cycle of unresolved anger, its effects, and the journey to uncover the root causes of rage. Breaking those patterns becomes easier once we identify them.

The weight of unresolved anger

Reflect on a memory that lingered in your mind like a broken record, one-sided and replaying repeatedly. Even minor things, like a word, look, or gesture, can leave a lasting impression on your emotional memory. We often ignore these slight issues, but they can escalate and become more bothersome. Before you realize it, your reactions are driven by the present and past emotional baggage.

Going through the same situations over and over again doesn't just affect our emotions; it can also damage our relationships, impact our work, and harm our health. Did you notice how stress makes you more likely to get sick or catch a cold? This is your body's message to break the cycle.

Identifying the root causes of anger

Breaking these patterns means digging deep into our minds to face what lies beneath. In this chapter, we'll continue with personal stories to see how past emotions affect present behavior. Let me introduce Dana, who figured out that work frustrations were more than just about the job.

Dana initially believed that her projects, tasks, and interactions with coworkers caused her anger. The intensity of her response didn't seem to match the reasons behind her feelings. The contrast sparked a deeper level of Dana's reflection regarding her motives. Thinking about herself, she realized that her anger came from being overlooked and unappreciated, with her efforts and contributions not being acknowledged or valued. This emotion wasn't unfamiliar; it had been present in her life since childhood.

Dana often felt invisible as a child. Growing up in a busy home with brothers who received more attention, she took her successes and failures personally. She chose to stay silent because she didn't think speaking up would make a difference. Hoping for recognition, she silently wished someone would notice her hard work. Throughout her life, she carried on the habit of seeking approval from her childhood, resulting in anger when she felt her efforts were not appreciated, especially at work.

When Dana understood this, her life transformed as she found new ways to handle her anger. It's like finding out that the song you can't get out of your head is an old one you didn't enjoy, and now you can finally switch to a different tune.

Breaking free

How can you break the cycle and begin a new journey? Follow these steps:

1. *Pay attention to how you feel.*

Start by being mindful of your feelings as they happen. Notice how your body reacts physically, like tightness in your chest, a clenched jaw, or a knot in your stomach. These are signals that your emotional experiences are about to resurface.

2. *Press pause.*

When you feel angry, take a break. As we previously discussed the effectiveness of pausing and deep breathing, I just want to remind you to try taking deep breaths, stepping away, or briefly closing your eyes. Pausing can stop you from reacting impulsively.

3. By *identifying your emotions*, you can lessen their intensity. Are you genuinely furious or experiencing hurt, disappointment, or fear? As we learned in chapter three, anger can be a way to protect ourselves from showing our vulnerable side and feelings.

4. *Express, don't suppress.*

Don't keep your feelings bottled up; find a healthy way to let them out. Some examples of self-care activities are talking to a friend, journaling, or exercising. Sharing your feelings provides an outlet to release emotional energy, preventing it from accumulating.

5. *Seek an understanding* of what is causing your anger. Past experiences and deeper issues often shape our reactions more than the current situation.

6. *Learn and practice new responses.*

Once you understand your triggers and root causes, explore new ways to respond. This might involve practicing mindfulness techniques, assertive communication, or taking breaks we've already covered.

Go to the workbook to understand the difference

between a reaction and a response.

7. *Strengthen your emotional resilience.*

To break the cycle of anger, work on building your inner toughness; this will improve your ability to cope with stress in life. You can build resilience through mindfulness meditation, regular exercise, and sufficient sleep.

Your unresolved anger

Now, let's get practical. Upon completing Chapter 6, "The Heavy Burden," where we uncovered the recurring cycle of unresolved anger, here are some thought-provoking questions for you.

1. *Identify patterns*: Think of a situation where you felt anger rising. Is this feeling familiar to you? Consider going back to when you first felt this way in similar situations. Can you identify any patterns?

2. *Understand triggers*: What specific words, actions, or events provoke your anger? Do these triggers remind you of past feelings or events you haven't fully addressed?

3. *Explore underlying emotions*: What emotions were you hiding behind your anger? Did you feel ignored, unappreciated, scared, or something else?

4. *Acknowledge needs*: What unmet needs surfaced in these moments of fury? How can you specifically meet those needs?

5. *Practice self-expression*: Reflect on your usual way of expressing anger. Is it hard for you to express your emotions before they become overwhelming? Why?

6. *Seek support*: Take a moment to think about your loved ones, close friends, and family. Who can you feel comfortable discussing your anger with?

7. *Learn and grow*: Analyzing your anger, what is one thing you've found out about yourself? How can you apply this knowledge to change your future responses?

8. *Choose a fresh path*: Now that you know more about your anger patterns, what's one thing you can do differently today to break the cycle?

Looking ahead

Understanding where our anger comes from and learning how to break its repetitive patterns can lead to a fresh start in our emotional growth. In the next chapter, "Raging Waves," we'll explore the power of emotional resilience and how you can harness it for yourself.

Before you turn to the next page, go to the workbook and read about the consequences of disregarding emotions, then complete the exercise there.

HUSHING THE STORM

7. Raging Waves

Let's say you just found out you didn't get the raise you worked so hard for. How do you feel? It feels like a storm has tossed your dreams and plans around, right?

At first, you might feel defeated and cling to the wreckage as waves of anger and sadness wash over you. Then you start to swim. You remember problems you've solved and times when you felt lost but found your way back to shore. You think about your abilities, your flexibility, and the people who are there for you and can help you. You begin to see this delay not as a loss but as a detour, a chance to change your plans and grow.

You've shown how tough you are because it wasn't just about surviving the storm. You did way more than that. You've learned to use the skills and strengths you've built up over the years. You know you can't change the weather, but you can adjust your sails, set an alternative course, and sail on. As a result, you feel more confident that you have what it takes to face life's challenges head-on rather than letting them overwhelm you. This chapter showcases ways to maintain your balance when things go wrong, using amazing thriving stories to bring the idea of resilience to life.

The power of emotional resilience

Navigating, there are times when the sea is quiet, which makes our trip easy and smooth. But every once in a while, storms happen that test our ability to keep the ship afloat and moving forward.

Emotional resilience helps us get through these rough times. Storms aren't something we can avoid; they're a part of our path. Instead, we can learn how to get through them and come out the other side, maybe a little wetter but wiser and more decisive.

Resilient people understand that rough seas are part of the journey. They see these challenges as opportunities to learn more about the world and themselves. Each storm they experience teaches valuable lessons and prepares them for the future.

Key characteristics of emotionally resilient people.

1. *Open to change.*

People who are resilient can adapt to new situations in the same way an expert sailor adjusts his sails when the wind changes. Their secret? A blend of creativity in problem-solving and a willingness to explore new ideas. Their agility helps them gracefully navigate uncertainty, showing that flexibility means actively adapting, not just enduring.

2. *Positive mindset.*

Maintaining a constructive attitude goes a long way. This doesn't mean pretending everything is fine when it's not. Instead of dwelling on the clouds, let's redirect our attention to what we can do and actively search for those moments of sunshine, even on the gloomiest days.

3. *Self-knowledge.*

It's like having a detailed blueprint of your strengths and weaknesses. When you know your emotions and the reasons behind them, you can better deal with challenging situations. Knowing when to ask for help or take a break is also essential.

4. *Perseverant.*

Resilient people do not give up, no matter how tough things get. They trust in themselves and diligently pursue their goals, regardless of the distance to the shore.

This determination shows the real essence of resilience — it's not just about getting through tough times but also about persistently moving ahead, even when the goal seems far away.

5. *Supportive and empathetic.*
Friends and family support is like having a crew on your boat. They can help steer, offer advice, or just be there to listen, making any journey easier and more enjoyable.

We can all work on developing emotional resilience over time. It involves consistently refining essential skills, extracting valuable lessons from our failures, and acknowledging that each difficulty contributes to our growth and knowledge.

Zenitude: Techniques for inner harmony

Trying to stay upright on a rocking ship is like maintaining balance in life's stormy moments. Like seasoned sailors with tactics for navigating rough seas, we can also develop techniques to stay balanced.
Allow me to share some practical methods that can assist you in maintaining control, even when facing overwhelming challenges.

1. Embrace mindfulness

Mindfulness is a practice rooted in ancient meditation traditions, particularly those found in Buddhism, but it has been popularized for widespread use in contemporary mental and physical health. At its core, mindfulness involves paying full attention to the present moment with openness, curiosity, and acceptance. It's about observing your thoughts, feelings, bodily sensations, and surrounding environment without judgment or reaction. When you use mindfulness techniques, you learn to observe your thoughts and feelings from a distance without getting swept up. Research has shown that mindfulness practice has numerous benefits, including the ability to manage difficult emotions such as anger and sadness through emotional regulation.

- *Try focused breathing.*

When you feel overwhelmed, take slow, deep breaths, inhaling through the nose for a count of four, holding for a count of four, and exhaling slowly through the mouth for a count of six. This technique helps activate the body's relaxation response and can be a quick fix to reduce immediate stress.

- *Use mindful observation.*

Focus on a single object within your sight. It could be a photo on the wall, a tree outside your window, or a pen on your desk. Notice only the details of the object — shape, color, texture— and allow yourself to be fully absorbed in observing them. This technique helps center the mind and distract it from sources of stress. It's like dropping an anchor in the middle of your day.

Being aware of what's going on in your body and mind is the fundamental aspect of mindfulness. It means noticing your physical sensations, thoughts, and feelings as they happen. This kind of awareness can help you spot the patterns in your behavior, like how you react when stressed or angry.

2. Cultivate a positive outlook

A positive outlook refers to the habit of maintaining a hopeful and optimistic attitude, focusing on the good aspects of any situation rather than dwelling on the negatives. This mindset involves expecting positive results, looking for solutions, and believing in your ability to overcome obstacles and challenges.

- *Keep a gratitude journal.*

Each night, write three things you're grateful for. It can be as simple as a sunny day, a great cup of coffee, or a kind smile from a stranger. It's all about training your brain to recognize the good stuff.

- *Challenge negative thoughts.*

When a dark thought enters your mind, ask yourself, "Is this really true?" or "Is there another way to look at this?"

Sometimes, our minds need a little nudge to see the light through the clouds.

3. Create a self-care routine

* *Schedule "Me Time."*

    Just as you'd schedule an important meeting, find time in your day for self-care. Whether it's taking a 15-minute walk, reading, or simply sitting quietly with a cup of tea amidst the daily rush.

* *Find your fun.*

    What makes you feel good? Dancing around your living room? Drawing? Baking? Ironing? Vacuuming? Do more of it. Fun isn't just for kids; it's vital to keeping our adult selves afloat.

4. Seek and offer support

* *Start a support group.*

    Create a group chat with friends or family to share the ups and downs. Sometimes, knowing you're not sailing alone can make all the difference.

* *Be a listening ear.*

    Offer to support someone else. It can be as simple as asking, "How are you doing?" and then listening to their answer. Helping others is a remarkable way of lifting one's spirits.

    Remember, maintaining balance doesn't mean suppressing anger or avoiding difficult situations. Instead, it's about arming yourself with the techniques to remain composed in the face of unexpected obstacles. And just like learning to sail, mastering this balance takes effort. The more you practice, the better equipped you'll be to navigate even the most severe storms with a little more grace.

Bounce back and thrive

As promised, I will share some amazing stories that inspired me in times of doubt. Even we psychologists have moments of vulnerability, which is my motivation for writing this book. I have found and used these strategies, first with myself and then with my clients. So, keep reading and practicing with the workbook. Now, let's dive into these incredibly inspiring stories.

Dr. Viktor Frankl, a neurologist, psychiatrist, and Holocaust survivor offers a profound example of emotional resilience through his experiences and insights detailed in his book "Man's Search for Meaning." Frankl survived three years in Nazi concentration camps, where he lost his parents, his brother, and his pregnant wife.

Despite these unimaginable losses and horrors he witnessed, Frankl gained a deep understanding of human resilience and the importance of finding meaning in all forms of existence, even the most brutal.

Frankl's psychological theory, known as logotherapy, is based on the belief that our primary drive in life is not pleasure (as Freud suggested) or power (as Adler stated) but the pursuit of what we find meaningful. During his time in the concentration camps, Frankl observed that those who could find meaning in their suffering were far more resilient to the physical and psychological torments they endured. He discovered that envisioning a future goal, such as reuniting with a loved one or finishing a job, gave people the strength to carry on under otherwise unbearable conditions.

After the war, Frankl returned to Vienna, where he continued his work as a therapist, helping patients find meaning in their suffering and thus a reason to go on living. His case is a powerful study of emotional resilience, demonstrating how finding meaning in the face of life's most tough challenges can provide the strength not only to survive but also to thrive. Frankl's life and work underscore the capacity of the human spirit to overcome adversity through the search for meaning, making him a classic example of resilience in psychology.

Then there's Mandy Harvey's story of pursuing her dreams despite seemingly insurmountable odds. A talented singer and songwriter, Mandy lost her hearing at the age of eighteen because of a connective tissue disorder, an event that could have ended her musical aspirations. However, Mandy's story is one of extraordinary determination and adaptability, showing her refusal to let her deafness silence her voice.

Before losing her hearing, Mandy was a promising music student, deeply connected to music from a young age and pursuing a degree in vocal music education. The loss of her hearing was devastating and caused her to put her musical dreams on hold. However, Mandy's passion for music never wavered. She found her way back to music with remarkable courage, learning to rely on muscle memory, visual tuners, and vibrations to sing and perform with precision.

Mandy's breakthrough came when she decided to audition for "America's Got Talent." There, she performed original songs and wowed the audience and judges with her beautiful voice and ability to perform flawlessly without hearing the music. Her performances were widely acclaimed, and she quickly became an inspiration to millions, proving that limitations can be overcome with creativity and perseverance.

Why these stories?

Each one highlights the importance of resilience. While resilience doesn't remove hardships, it equips us to navigate through them and come out stronger. Finding meaning in suffering can transform a personal tragedy into an opportunity for growth. Purpose can fuel resilience by providing a compass through our darkest moments. What we may perceive as limitations can offer unique advantages and perspectives. Embracing and capitalizing on these can result in significant breakthroughs and impactful contributions.

Adaptability is a cornerstone of resilience and personal growth. It's never too late to pursue our dreams, as obstacles can be overcome with creativity, perseverance, and passion. Pursuing what we love brings fulfillment and joy that transcend challenges. Change begins with believing in ourselves and our cause. Self-belief empowers us to advocate for ourselves and others, even in the face of formidable opposition.

Vulnerability is a strength, not a weakness. Embracing vulnerability can lead to deeper connections with others, greater self-awareness, and an authentic life. True success isn't just about personal accolades or achievements; it's more about our impact on the lives of others and the world around us. These inspiring stories and many more illuminate the path through life's stormy seas, teaching us that with resilience, purpose, and a willingness to embrace our unique selves and vulnerabilities, we can overcome any hardship and use it to break through limitations.

Exploring your emotional resilience

Reading these stories of strength and seeing how each person kept their balance despite the challenges can help us see the strength we already have but haven't used.

As a psychologist, I've heard many stories like this, and, likely, similar turning points in your life have quietly made you stronger. This chapter has sparked my creativity, and I now have a list of questions that will guide your inner exploration.

1. *Reflect on your resilience.* Think about when you faced a challenging situation or experienced a loss. How did you initially react, and how did you manage to move past it?

2. *Identify your anchors.* What things do you rely on to stay calm during challenging times? These can include mindfulness practices, hobbies, routines, or relationships.

3. *Embrace change.* Have you ever had a loss that opened doors to new passions or opportunities? How did it change the way you saw the challenges you went through?

4. *Seek support.* Who supports you, and how do you reach out to them when things get difficult? How do you assist others when they're in need?

5. *Practice self-compassion.* How do you take care of yourself and show kindness during challenging times?

6. *Cultivate a positive outlook.* Take a moment to think about how you usually address problems or setbacks. How would a more positive outlook on life affect your approach to these problems?

7. *Try mindfulness.* If you've practiced meditation or mindfulness, how has it helped you manage your emotions during highs and lows? If not, what's holding you back from trying it?

From now on, remember that resilience is a skill that can be learned, not something you're born with. With every challenge, we can improve this ability.

Looking ahead

As we enter the next chapter, "The Crossroads," we remember the fantastic lessons from Mandy and Frankl. They show us that we always have choices when dealing with problems and that we can transform them into opportunities.

Let's keep these stories close to our hearts as we meet our next crossroads, knowing that with strength, help, and a little courage, we can find our way to a future full of hope and possibility.

Within the pages of this book, you discover a blend of motivational ingredients that, I hope, kindle your spirit. Given my background as a positive psychologist, I'm a powerful advocate of the idea that our attitudes play a crucial role in determining our actions. Embracing positivity empowers us to create stronger connections with the world, while negativity acts as a barrier, hampering our ability to connect and limiting our perspectives.

Blend the insights with motivation, absorb them deeply, and let them shape you into a fearless version of yourself.

HUSHING THE STORM

8. The Crossroads

Close your eyes and imagine yourself at a decisive moment in your career, faced with a choice: a safe, financially rewarding job that fails to ignite your passion or a risky yet exciting opportunity to start your venture and pursue the dreams that light your soul. The safe path may offer comfort and stability, but the mere thought of it evokes a deep sense of dread, a reminder of the fantastic possibilities that await elsewhere. On the other hand, taking a risky path is full of challenges and uncertainty, but it also brings the excitement of chasing your dream.

In this moment, the incredible power of choice becomes clear. What would you choose?

The same applies to anger. When you are caught in the heat of the moment, but before reacting, it is like standing at a crossroads in the middle of a vast, breathtaking landscape. One path takes you through familiar territory, where anger leads your journey, whipping up whirlwinds and leaving a trail of resentment. What about the other path? It may seem unfamiliar, but it promises a trip where you hold the compass, guiding your steps with thoughtfulness and care, even as anger obscures your vision. In this chapter, I invite you to discover the incredible power of choice and to learn how to use that power to create a journey that's both peaceful and empowering.

From rage to reason: The power of choice

Have you ever felt a storm of anger brewing inside you, with thunder, lightning, and rain pouring down? It might feel like the only choice during those moments is to release everything, similar to a summer thunderstorm. Here's a little secret: you have the superpower of your choice. Imagine having a magical umbrella that shields you from your heated feelings.

Picture yourself in one of those critical moments when the storm of anger is about to break. Instead of surrendering to the pouring rain, you remember your extraordinary umbrella — the power to decide. You take a deep breath, open it wide, and ponder, *"Wait! Is there another way I can handle this? Do I have to let the storm take over?"* This doesn't mean the storm isn't happening or you ignore the thunder and lightning. It simply means you are choosing not to get caught in the rain.

This remarkable power of choice doesn't make the anger storm disappear. No, it's still there. But it lets you decide how you react, which is pretty cool. Instead of letting anger control you and making you say or do things you might regret (like getting wet without an umbrella), you can choose how you respond. Instead of acting impulsively, consider taking a walk, talking to a friend, or simply relaxing and letting the storm pass. Don't get caught in the heat of the moment!

So, the next time you feel a storm coming, remember your magical umbrella and your power of choice. It's always there, right in your hand, ready to help you stay dry and navigate the storm on your terms. But who knows? With practice, you might become the best storm navigator there is, guiding yourself through with confidence and maybe even helping others find their way.

A guide to the pause and reflect technique

Okay, let's talk about a cool trick I have for you called the Pause and Reflect technique. We've talked about pausing before, but now let's break down why it's beneficial to use it.

Imagine it as your superpower, like having a pause button to freeze time when overwhelmed, making a big difference in handling anger. Here's a simplified breakdown in two steps:

1. *Press pause*

Imagine watching your favorite show when something big is about to happen, but you hit the pause button because you have to get some popcorn. This is how you deal with your emotions when you get angry. Instead of letting the scene play out and possibly end in a way you didn't want (like yelling or saying something you might regret), you hit the imaginary pause button. Take a deep breath...and maybe another.

2. *Time to reflect*

Now that you've paused, it's time to do some detective work. Ask yourself important questions, such as "*What is at the heart of my anger?*" and "*What do I really hope to get out of this situation?*". This is like taking a step back and looking at the big picture rather than just the part bothering you. Maybe someone hurt you, or your frustration stems from feeling unheard.

When you identify what's truly bothering you, you can choose a thoughtful rather than an impulsive response.

Why it's incredibly useful?

The Pause and Reflect technique is beautiful because it allows you to regain control. Instead of letting anger drive the bus, you're back in the driver's seat, deciding where you want to go.

The next time you feel the simmering heat of anger rising, reach for your secret weapon: stop, take several deep breaths, and engage in a thoughtful dialogue with yourself. *"What's happening here, and how can I handle it in a way I'll be proud of?"*

This technique is valuable not just in the heat of the moment but can also be improved with practice. The more you use it, the easier it gets; soon, you'll be able to handle difficult emotional situations with confidence. So, give it a try! You might be surprised at how helpful pausing and reflecting can be.

The decision lab for better choices

We've all been there — standing at a crossroads, needing to make a big decision — but our anger is getting in the way. Those heated emotions can mess with our rational minds, making it hard to trust our judgment. But here are some strategies that can help you make better decisions, especially when angry.

1. Pros and cons list with an emotional twist

This exercise is a smart way to make decisions, combining logical analysis and emotional intelligence. The traditional pros and cons list is refined by adding introspection, which boosts emotional depth to each decision component.

- *Create your list.*

Start by drawing a two-column table. Label one column "Pros" and the other "Cons." List all the logical reasons for and against the decision you're considering.

- *Add an emotional twist.*

Next to each pro and con, add a small note about how you feel. Is there excitement or dread? Confidence or fear? Be as honest as you can.

- *Evaluate the emotional responses.*

Once you've listed the emotional responses next to the logical items, take a moment to review them. Pay special attention to any items that evoke a strong emotional reaction.

- *Investigate why.*

For each item that evokes a strong emotional response, ask yourself why that might be. What about this particular pro or con touches a deeper part of your psyche? Is it tied to past experiences, hopes for the future, or perhaps an unacknowledged fear or desire?

You can achieve a more balanced view of the decision by identifying your emotional reactions to each pro and con. This balance is crucial because decisions made with either too much emotion or too much rationality may not lead to the most fulfilling results. Emotional evaluation can reveal biases you weren't aware of, such as a tendency to choose paths that seem safer but are less aligned with your genuine desires. This exercise guides you to make decisions that are not only logical but also in harmony with your emotional well-being. It promotes a comprehensive approach to decision-making, where you make choices fully aware of their influence on your life and happiness.

2. The role-reversal debate

This dynamic exercise encourages people to imagine themselves in other people's shoes, especially in situations where opinions are strongly divided. It increases empathy, broadens perspectives, and improves decision-making skills. This exercise is particularly helpful in understanding complex situations and resolving conflicts.

- *Identify the issue.*

Begin by identifying the decision or conflict at hand. Clearly define the different viewpoints or options available. The problem must involve a difference of opinion, which sets the stage for meaningful discussion.

- *Choose opposing sides.*

Assign roles based on opposing viewpoints. If you're doing this exercise alone, you'll take on both roles, one after the other. Participants can pair or assign roles in a group setting to represent different perspectives.

- *Prepare your arguments.*

Each participant (or you, if practicing alone) prepares underlying facts for that assigned perspective. This includes researching and formulating coherent points that support the position, even if they contradict personal beliefs.

- *Engage in the debate.*

Participants present their arguments and defend their positions while listening to and considering the opposing side. The goal is not to "win" the debate but to fully explore and articulate the reasoning behind each perspective.

- *Reflect on the experience.*

Once the debate is done, take a moment to consider what it was like to argue from a different viewpoint. Discuss or journal any new insights you gained, whether it was challenging to defend the opposing view, and how the exercise changed your understanding of the issue.

By advocating a different perspective, you can gain a valuable understanding of others' thoughts and feelings, encouraging you to examine overlooked or dismissed aspects of the argument.

This exercise challenges your cognitive flexibility and can shift rigid thought patterns. It supports the development of open-mindedness and adaptability.

3. The 5-5-5 Rule

Another great one to try is the 5-5-5 rule, a simple yet powerful decision-making framework designed to help individuals navigate the complexities of choice by considering the impact of their decisions in three distinct time frames: the immediate, the mid-term, and the long-term future. This rule encourages you to evaluate how you will feel about a decision 5 minutes or hours, 5 months, and 5 years from now.

- *Immediate consequences* (5 minutes, 5 hours).

First, consider the immediate impact of your decision. How will you feel about this decision in 5 minutes or 5 hours? This step will help you determine your emotional response and the short-term impact of your action, allowing you to assess whether it is consistent with your immediate needs and values.

- *Medium-term impact* (5 months).

Next, imagine yourself five months into the future. How will this decision affect your life at that time? This timeframe allows you to evaluate the sustainability of the decision and its alignment with your mid-term goals and plans. It's a balance between the impulsive desires of the moment and your long-term aspirations.

- *Long-term consequences* (5 years).

Finally, imagine your life 5 years after you make this decision. What long-term impact will it have on your life, relationships, and personal growth? This perspective encourages you to consider the decision's impact and its consistency with the life you want to live.

The 5-5-5 rule helps you clarify what's truly important to you by considering the implications of your choices, bringing your core values into focus, and guiding you toward decisions that align with those values. I think it's a well-organized framework that helps keep a balance between emotional impulses and rational thinking. I lean on this framework in my personal and professional life, and it helps me navigate various situations.

If you think about how you will feel about a decision in the future, you are more likely to make emotionally satisfying choices based on logic.

4. The stop and decide technique

This mindful decision-making strategy emphasizes the importance of pausing deliberately before responding to a situation, especially when emotions are running high. Based on mindfulness and emotional regulation principles, this technique advocates a moment of introspection to prevent rash decisions and promote a more thoughtful and deliberate approach to life's challenges.

- *The need to stop.*

The first step is to recognize the signs that you're becoming emotionally charged or facing a decision that requires careful consideration. This could be stress, anger, confusion, or simply the awareness that you are at an important point in your life.

- *Take a physical step back.*

If possible, distance yourself from the situation. This might mean stepping away from a conversation, shutting down your laptop, or simply closing your eyes and focusing inward.

- *Engage in mindful breathing.*

Focus on your breath and take slow, deep breaths to calm your mind and body. Mindful breathing serves as an anchor, bringing you into the present moment and away from the immediacy of your emotional reactions.

- *Reflect on the situation.*

With a calmer state of mind, reflect on the problem at hand. Ask yourself key questions: What are the facts? What emotions am I feeling, and why? What are the potential outcomes of my responses?

Consider how your different options align with your long-term values and goals. This can serve as a guide to help you make choices that align with your overall aspirations and principles.

- *Decide on a course of action.*

After taking the time to pause and reflect, make a thoughtful decision that aligns with your best self. Sometimes, this process may lead you to seek more information or advice before acting.

Pausing before you react makes you less likely to make impulsive decisions you may regret later. This is especially valuable in emotionally charged situations where the first impulse may not be the best response. Regularly practicing this technique can improve your ability to manage emotions, leading to greater emotional awareness. It also promotes mindfulness by focusing on the present moment, which can reduce stress and anxiety. With a calm and more balanced mindset, your decisions are more likely to be thoughtful and well-considered, showing a deeper understanding of the situation and its potential impact.

Reflecting on your values and goals during this process ensures your actions are more consistently aligned with what is truly important to you.

5. The worst-case scenario analysis

While we're talking about this, I should share one more method with you. This cognitive strategy helps individuals manage anxiety and fear related to decision-making and future planning. In this technique, we identify the worst probable outcome that could result from a particular decision or action, then systematically assess the likelihood of that outcome and plan how to cope with or mitigate it if it occurs. By confronting fears directly and rationally, we can reduce the power these fears have over our decision-making processes.

- *Describe the decision or situation.*

Begin by clearly defining the decision or situation causing anxiety or fear. We need to know precisely what you're worried about in order to address your concerns.

- *Identify the worst-case scenario.*

Think about the worst thing that could happen because of this decision or situation. Be specific about this scenario, even if it feels uncomfortable or exaggerated.

- *Rate the probability.*

Once you have identified the worst-case scenario, evaluate how likely it will happen. Use evidence and experience to assess the likelihood rather than letting fear dictate your perception.

- *Develop coping strategies.*

Consider how you would cope or respond if the worst-case scenario were to occur. What resources, support systems, or actions could you rely on to manage or mitigate the situation? Making plans for the worst can help you feel in charge and ready.

- *Consider preventive measures.*

Identify any steps you can take to reduce the likelihood of the worst-case scenario occurring. This may include gathering more information, seeking advice, or taking specific actions to prevent the feared outcome.

- *Reevaluate the decision.*

With a clearer understanding of the worst-case scenario, its likelihood, and how to deal with it, reevaluate the original decision or situation. Often, this process reveals that the feared outcome is either highly unlikely or manageable, reducing anxiety and allowing for rational decision-making.

By directly addressing fears and anxieties, this technique can significantly reduce the stress associated with uncertainty and the unknown, making it easier to decide. Identifying coping strategies and preventative measures improves problem-solving skills and encourages proactive rather than reactive thinking. By demystifying fear and providing a structured approach to assessing risk, this technique can make the decision-making process more transparent and less daunting, leading to more confident and informed choices.

With some practice, you'll be able to stop, take a breath, and make fair decisions, even when anger is brewing. These skills not only diffuse outrage at the moment but also prevent regrettable choices that you'll look back on with frustration. You're not just walking down an old path; you're forging a new one.

These exercises develop helpful skills to support you in all aspects of life. You'll avoid anger traps by practicing to stop, reflect, and choose the best path forward.

 Use the workbook to personalize these techniques and experience the transformative effect they can have. Simply scan the code for the workbook.

Who knew a simple pause could be so powerful?

HUSHING THE STORM

9. The Reflection

Imagine stepping into a room filled with soft, warm light, with a large, beautiful mirror at its center. This is no ordinary mirror; it's a special one that reveals your physical appearance and inner self. I highly recommend that you do the exercise in the workbook, a simple self-awareness technique that will reveal much about how you see yourself and how your friends see you. It could be a great starting point to help you build self-confidence. It's a small step, but it is a jump in the right direction for self-awareness.

As we continue our journey, in this chapter, we focus on standing in front of that mirror and recognizing our anger as an external event and an internal part of ourselves that we can understand, learn from, and grow with.

The role of self-awareness

We can define self-awareness as the ability to connect with yourself and understand your emotions and motivations. It's like holding a map in your hand, but instead of showing roads and cities, it shows your emotional landscape. It's fascinating, isn't it?

Let me share a little backstory about Samantha, a compassionate high school teacher who noticed a growing sense of irritability within herself in the classroom. She was known for her calm and thoughtful attitude, but she was concerned about her tendency to become irritable and to react harshly to her students' questions and mistakes. This behavior change affected relationships with her students and her confidence as an educator. After a few therapy sessions, Samantha took some time to reflect on her recent actions. She started a daily routine of keeping a reflective journal, concentrating on events that triggered anger or frustration throughout the day. Then, openly discuss the situations, her reactions, and any thoughts or feelings that arose during those moments.

While on this journey of self-reflection, Samantha realized her frustration was not aimed at her students. Instead, it came from her deep sense of duty towards her students' achievements and anxiety about the upcoming standardized tests. She discovered she had absorbed this pressure, leading to feelings of frustration towards minor classroom disruptions or questions, perceiving them as obstacles to her students' learning.

Now, imagine you standing in front of that mirror, looking deeply into your emotional world. This is not always easy, but it is imperative. As you become more familiar with this emotional reflection of yourself, you will notice certain things that cause your anger to flare up. It's like discovering which roads on your map lead to Thunder City and deciding to take a different route next time.

Here's where the magic happens: as you continue looking in that mirror, you'll find more than anger. Just like Samantha, you may discover hidden truths such as fear or sadness masquerading as anger, perhaps because these emotions find the guise of rage more comfortable.

What does it all mean to you? Make your Emotional Map.

- *Start with your triggers.*

Knowing what causes your anger allows you to prepare for, or even avoid, those triggers. It's like marking dangerous areas on a map so you can navigate around them. Make a list of your triggers.

- *Recognize your patterns.*

You'll begin to notice how you typically react when you're angry. Do you raise your voice? Do you become silent?

Understanding these patterns is like knowing if you're about to take a highway of anger or a peaceful byway. Add these to your map.

• *Add peaceful routes.*

Above all, ensure that this self-awareness map has pathways that bring you to peace. Maybe it's talking it out, taking a few deep breaths, or going for a walk. We've covered many techniques for finding calm in previous chapters. Choose the ones that work for you and put them on your map. Use the guide in the workbook.

Inner mirror

Exploring your mind and being open to personal growth is exciting, like an adventure. This trip may bring surprises and challenges, but in the end, it's gratifying. I'll give you tools and tips to help you dive into your emotions instead of just scratching the surface.

1. *The feeling wheel*

Imagine a big, colorful wheel like the ones you see at carnivals, but instead of prizes, each section is labeled with a particular emotion. There are basic emotions like happiness, sadness, and anger, but more complex ones like gratitude, loneliness, or hope.

Every day, or whenever you're feeling a little lost in

your emotions, spin this wheel in your head and see where it lands. It's a super fun way to get specific about your feelings. In the workbook, you'll find a ready-to-use feeling wheel and a handy guide to help you make the most of it.

Let's sketch one: Draw a large circle on paper and divide it into slices, like a pizza. In each slice, write different emotions; try to include a mix of positive, negative, and neutral feelings like happiness, sadness, anger, surprise, and fear, as well as more nuanced ones like gratitude, loneliness, insecurity, fear, excitement, or anticipation.

Look at the wheel when you're stressed or unsure how you feel. Identify what emotion(s) you're experiencing. This picture helps you name and recognize your feelings, which is the first step to understanding yourself.

2. *Emotional temperature checks*

Throughout the day, take quick "temperature checks" of your emotions. Ask yourself, "On a scale of 1 to 10, how calm or agitated am I right now?" This can help you see if your emotional temperature rises, which may show that it's time to cool down or address something bothering you.

Implement the checks: Evaluate your emotional state three times a day (morning, noon, and night). Use your phone to set reminders.

Record: On a scale from 1 (calm) to 10 (intense), rate your emotional "temperature" when the alarm goes off. Write about what's going on or how you feel right now. Over the next few weeks, you'll notice trends that will help you better prepare for and handle emotional changes.

3. *The mindful minute*

Take a minute — literally, just 60 seconds — a few times a day to practice mindfulness. You can focus on your breath, the surrounding sounds, or how your body feels in the moment. This mini mental break can help you center yourself, making it easier to reflect on your emotions and reactions from a calm place.

Build the habit. Choose specific triggers throughout the day to practice mindfulness, like waiting for your coffee to brew or right before starting the car, brushing your teeth, starting the computer, or going to bed.

Add variety. During each mindful minute, focus on different senses. One day, focus on what you hear; another, focus on what you feel in your body. This practice brings you into the present, reduces stress, and increases self-awareness, which is the secret to self-management.

4. *Emotional games*

Give it a try, even though it might seem strange. Show your recent emotions through non-verbal actions, alone or with a trusted person. Through this exercise, you can have fun exploring your feelings and learn more about how they show up for you.

Set the stage. Find a quiet, comfortable place where no one will bother you. Pick an emotion that you've had lately. Make sure the person you're with is someone you trust a lot.

Act it out. Show how you feel without using words. Pay attention to how your body moves, what you do with your face, and how you feel inside.

Reflect. Once you've expressed the emotion, spend some time exploring how it made you feel, the thoughts that accompanied it, and why it's surfacing at this moment. This can help you understand how your feelings live in your mind and body.

The compliment sandwich

When you need to work on experiences or issues involving someone else, use the compliment sandwich reflection method. Start with something positive about the person or situation, address the problem or emotion that bothers you, and end on a positive note. This method frames your thoughts constructively and allows you to focus on solutions rather than simply dwelling on problems.

Preparation: Before dealing with a problem, take a moment to write the positive aspects and things you appreciate about the person or situation. This will give you a more well-rounded perspective on the discussion.

Application: This technique isn't just for conversations with others; use it in your journal, too. For example, "(positive)

I love how dedicated I am to my projects, but (problem) *I get frustrated when I procrastinate.* (positive) *I'm proud of myself for wanting to do better.*" Use this structure in your journal to reflect on a conflict or difficult situation. Writing it can help you clarify your thoughts and feelings before communicating them to others.

Each tool has its way of helping you connect with your emotions while making them uncomplicated and explicit. Introducing them into your daily life will inspire you to delve into your thoughts and uncover valuable discoveries. Remember, self-reflection is about being curious, compassionate, and open to your inner world. So, like an emotional explorer, grab your hat, and let's continue exploring.

Self-discovery questions

Going deep into our feelings, especially anger, is like joining a treasure hunt where the prize is getting to know ourselves better. Let's use the mirror again — the one that reflects your emotions, thoughts, and heart pattern — and imagine you standing in front of it. What do you see?

Do you understand what makes you tick, especially with anger? Here are some simple ways to explore your emotional mirror.

Discover the layers beneath your anger. What are you really angry about?

Insight: Think of anger as the tip of an iceberg. There's usually something bigger underneath, like hurt, fear, or frustration. It's the same when you're angry because the dishes aren't done, but deep down, you feel unappreciated.

Learn to recognize your anger patterns. How do you usually react when angry?

Insight: Do you yell, remain silent, or perhaps comment sarcastically? Noticing your go-to response is like finding your emotional fingerprint — it is uniquely yours, and recognizing it is the first step before choosing a different reaction.

What triggers you? What patterns do you notice?

Insight: Are there certain situations or people that ignite your anger? It could be as specific as morning traffic or as complex as conversations about finances. Identifying these triggers is like marking a map with "Here Be Dragons" so you can navigate more carefully next time.

Understand your anger's effects. How does your anger affect your relationships?

Insight: Do you and your loved ones feel closer or further apart after a tempest of anger? It's like checking the weather after a storm to see if it's sunny or if there's damage that needs to be repaired.

Change the patterns. What changes do you want to make and where (what behavior or chain of thought)?
Insight: As you reflect on your journey with anger, what are you proud of, and what areas do you feel you could improve? Perhaps you've made progress in expressing your feelings, yet you still find it difficult to calm down when you become heated. It's like reviewing your travel journal and planning your next adventure.

When you dive into these questions, you're not just staring at your reflection; you're having a real heart-to-heart with yourself. Imagine treating your emotional mirror with the same warmth and interest you'd show a good friend.

The journey of self-reflection can be difficult, but, oh, is it rewarding?

Getting to the bottom of why we feel angry and understanding those triggers and patterns gives us a choice in how we respond. And with that choice comes stronger bonds, a better understanding of who we are, and a calmer, more peaceful life. How great is that?

CALM WATERS

10. Healing Hearts

Let's imagine that with each page of this book, we have been together on a long sea voyage, crossing the high tides of understanding anger. Now, we've reached calm waters and clear skies — a perfect place for a pause and some much-needed rest. In this peaceful setting, let's explore the power of forgiveness and how it can be like a healing balm for our hearts when we forgive ourselves.

What exactly is forgiveness? Letting go.

Yes, it is releasing resentment, hatred, bitterness, or the desire to get even with someone who has hurt us. Letting go doesn't mean forgetting what happened or pretending the hurt didn't matter. It did and still does because the impact of the wrongdoing is real, and it's essential to acknowledge and express it.

Forgiveness is all about choosing to release the grip these negative emotions have on us by saying, "*I refuse to let this fury control my life any longer.*" I warmly recommend using the workbook to uncover your inner world of resentment and start the work on healing.

Letting go

Picture holding a hot coal, ready to throw it at someone who has hurt you. The longer you hold it, the more it burns you. The pain intensifies, and yet, letting go feels impossible. It's not easy — holding onto these feelings can be like clutching a shield, protecting you from further pain. But in reality, this shield often becomes a burden, weighing you down and keeping you trapped in a cycle of negativity.

Letting go is the act of opening your hand to drop the coal. It brings relief to you, not to the person who caused you pain. **Understanding that holding onto anger and resentment harms you the most is a powerful act of self-care, courage, and love**.

Why does forgiveness heal?

Forgiveness shifts your focus from dwelling on past wounds to how you'll deal with them in the future. This shift doesn't erase the pain or suggest that the hurt is acceptable. It means you acknowledge your suffering but refuse to let it define you. Forgiveness is all about reclaiming your power and deciding that your happiness and peace are worth more than the pain someone else caused. When you forgive, you reclaim your power and take control of your emotional well-being. You give yourself the gift of freedom to heal, grow, and live fully.

When you forgive, you fill your emotional wounds with compassion and understanding, like treating a physical wound with a healing salve. This inner healing process eases your pain from within, allowing you to move forward with a lighter heart and a clearer mind.

Release the hold.

Holding onto unforgiveness can make you feel suffocated. It consumes your thoughts, disrupts your sleep, and even affects your physical health, like being in a stuffy room with no air, feeling trapped and stifled. But forgiveness is like opening a window in that room, letting in fresh air, and invigorating you with new energy and perspective.

Choosing to forgive is a conscious decision not to let your pain dictate your happiness or how you live your life. It's deciding that you deserve peace and joy, even in the face of past hurts.

Moving forward

When you forgive, you take the most important step toward healing by choosing freedom. It frees you from the relentless cycle of anger and retribution, paving the way for peace and emotional health. Reclaiming your control from those who have wronged you and deciding that their actions won't cause more pain is a powerful choice.

Self-forgiveness is the starting point.

Forgiving ourselves can sometimes feel like trying to climb Mount Everest with no gear. It's challenging, exhausting, and sometimes seems impossible. We relive our mistakes repeatedly, and with each replay, the feelings of guilt or regret deepen, making it seem like we're suffocating.

But what if we flipped the script? What if we treated ourselves with the same kindness and understanding we would give to a friend at the time of a blunder? See yourself being there for your best friend when they confess a mistake. You wouldn't criticize them or hold it over their heads, would you? Instead, you'd offer a listening ear, your presence, and perhaps a pep talk to remind them that perfection is unfeasible and idealistic.

Imagine extending the same kindness to yourself. We need to recognize that we are all humans prone to stumbling and wishing for do-overs. Forgiving means allowing yourself to drop the weight you've been carrying. There's immense liberation in acknowledging that you did your best with what you knew then.

Learning from those missteps and moving forward with a lighter heart is the essence of forgiveness.

Freedom is in distancing from others, too

Holding onto our anger toward others is like trekking with a heavy backpack; it slows you down and makes each step harder. Choosing to distance yourself from those who hurt you is like letting go of that burden. Suddenly, you can breathe more freely, walk more lightly, and appreciate the journey. Forgiving doesn't mean you have to trust or keep them in your life. It means you've chosen the distance to release the weight of anger for your own sake, not theirs.

Learn how to forgive

Forgiveness is a deeply personal and transformative journey. I'll help you through this process by making sure you can connect with each step in a meaningful way, touching on your emotions.

1. Acknowledge your pain

Accept and embrace your emotions regarding the harm you've experienced and its impact on your life. It's okay to feel hurt, angry, or betrayed. These feelings are there, and they deserve recognition to come out. That is how you feel. Say it out loud!

2. *Express your fury, resentment, and grudge*

Holding these emotions inside can be toxic, leading to emotional and physical stress. Whether it's through talking with a trusted friend, writing in a journal, or even engaging in physical activity like running or punching a pillow. In my experience as a psychologist, this part usually takes up the most energy and time for healing. When you let these emotions out, you're not just venting; you're releasing the hurt that has been holding you down. This feeling of release is one of the most liberating steps you will experience before deciding to forgive.

3. *Have the closure you need for that hurtful event*

Healing is a choice, and it's one that only you can make. Maybe it is challenging going back to feeling powerless, but making that choice is a gift to yourself and a way to take control of your well-being.

If you find it difficult to deal with those emotions, consider seeking help from a therapist to safely process the event. Don't let someone else's actions define you, but be open to receiving support to heal.

For the hurt to fade, you need to visualize a closure to that event, which empowers you and makes you take control and change the emotional echo. The end can also be that you let the event fade in the past with all the hurt that caused you. The closure will bring you inner peace and emotional freedom.

4. *Feel safe and let go*

Feeling safe in the present moment is the secret your body needs to let go of resentment and bitterness. It takes effort and the willingness to do it every single day. Meditation, writing, or just talking about what happened and your choice to let go can be very beneficial. These activities help you work through your feelings and remind you that the past is behind and the present is safe.

Think of it like putting down a heavy backpack you've been lugging around for years. The feeling of relief and lightness is instant. By letting go, you're freeing yourself from all that emotional weight.

5. *Heal and grow*

Imagine a tree that a storm has scarred. The tempest may have damaged its branches, but it also made the tree's roots grow deeper and stronger. Similarly, your experiences can deepen your resilience, no matter how painful. When you forgive, you acknowledge the pain, hurt, and lessons from those experiences. Each act of forgiveness carries with it a wealth of insights and wisdom. Maybe you've learned about your boundaries, the importance of self-respect, or the strength you possess to overcome adversity. These lessons are invaluable; they shape your character and enrich your understanding of life.

Picture your heart as a garden. Forgiveness is like tending to this garden, pulling out the weeds of resentment and anger, and planting seeds of compassion and understanding. As you nurture these seeds, they grow into beautiful flowers, filling your life with color, joy, and peace. The act of forgiveness cultivates an environment where your emotional well-being can flourish.

Forgiveness brings an undeniable sense of peace. It's the quiet confidence that comes from knowing you are in control of your emotions. This peace is not just a fleeting moment of relief but a lasting state of being that infuses every aspect of your life. Living peacefully means approaching life's challenges with a clear mind and a calm heart. It helps you handle conflicts with grace and understanding, making it easier to deal with the emotional ups and downs that used to be so overwhelming.

Forgiving can take a long time, so be patient and kind to yourself along the way. Putt the balm on gently, let it do its job, and notice how slowly but surely the wound heals.

If you're struggling, seek the help of a local therapist who specializes in treating trauma. They will be with you every step of the way, ensuring that you don't experience any unnecessary pain.

As you move forward, remember that forgiving yourself is one of the bravest and most loving things you can do. Go to the workbook for a helpful guide on this journey.

Forgiveness is like a natural healing remedy we should all embrace. It's a way of living that helps us grow, find inner peace, and love ourselves more. While the famous Balm of Gilead healed people's wounds, forgiveness can heal our own. It can also make the world kinder, compassionate, and connected. Wouldn't that make the world a better place?

CALM WATERS

11. Bridging Angry Hearts

Let's talk about the people closest to us — the ones who see us lose it when we're mad and the ones who are there for us when a slight irritation turns into a full-blown storm. We need to be aware of our tantrums' impact on the people we care about, sometimes leaving wounds that can't be seen but last long after the anger is gone.

Take a look at Marco's story; it may resonate with you. Marco was sitting at his desk. The room was getting darker, and the computer screen's glow was all that was visible. Deadlines, meetings, and an ever-growing to-do list ran through his mind. As the day passed, a nagging thought came to light: he had promised Elena that he would stop by a restaurant on his way home and buy dinner.

An important email from his boss that required immediate attention quickly drowned out the thought. The weight of his work stress overshadowed Marco's promise to Elena when he finally turned off his computer. It wasn't until he saw the disappointment in her eyes that the memory resurfaced, sharp and accusing.

At that moment, Marco felt a surge of frustration — not at Elena, but at himself and the situation. Elena stood before him, her face a mirror of his exhaustion and frustration. "*Why can't you just understand that I've had a rough day?*" he found himself saying, the words coming out in a desperate attempt to hide his guilt. Even as he spoke, a part of him flinched, recognizing the unfairness of his response. Elena's hurt expression only deepened his sense of remorse. Still, the cycle of stress and misdirected anger had already taken hold, driving a wedge into the evening that was supposed to be their sanctuary from the outside world.

Marco was becoming increasingly aware of this pattern: He would vent his anger at Elena, not because she was to blame but because she made him feel safe enough to show his weaknesses. This was both comforting and challenging to realize.

In the quiet that followed their fight, Marco thought about how strange it was that the person he

loved most was also the one who was unintentionally getting his worst feelings. He decided to change that.

Can you relate to Marco's story? Maybe it's not in the same context, but do you recognize the feeling? Think about it: We often express our anger and frustration around those we love deeply — our partners, children, parents, or best friends. It's as if we reserve our most intense, unguarded emotions for those who mean the world to us while presenting a calm exterior to everyone else.

This chapter serves as a heartfelt ode to those who stand by us, showing patience and unconditional support through our emotional upheavals.

If these words resonate with you, I encourage you to share this book with your loved ones, be they your partner, siblings, children, or dearest friends. Pause now for a moment and tell them you know how your anger may have affected them and that you're determined to make changes so your relationships are lasting.

I encourage you to read this chapter together and use the workbook to deepen your connection, revealing more about who you are.

Dealing with anger in relationships

When the people we care about get angry, it can be difficult to figure out the best way to support them. I understand, and that's why I wrote this chapter. It's all about showing you how to be there for your loved ones with empathy, patience, and a lot of heart. Together, we'll explore ways to listen actively, offer support, and stay present while managing your emotional well-being.

Recognizing anger in those close to us can sometimes feel like trying to read a map in dim light. It's not always as straightforward as raised voices or furrowed brows. More often, subtle changes, like quiet shifts in behavior or mood, hint at anger brewing beneath the surface. Let's shed some light on recognizing these signs and understanding the more profound messages they may share.

The subtle signs of anger

Rage does not always appear with a bang in those closest to us. Sometimes, it's in silence — a withdrawal from conversations they usually enjoy or a loss of interest in activities that used to bring them joy.

It's like noticing someone who always wears long sleeves to hide a bruise; the signs are there, but they're covered up and not visible.

For more details, review Chapter 1.

1. Changes in communication

Notice how they communicate. An angry person may speak softer or louder. Their jokes may have a bite, and their comments are often laced with sarcasm. It's as if their words have been dipped in a slightly bitter sauce, affecting the conversation's flavor. You may notice that it's a recent change or a recurring one.

2. Physical clues

Anger can also manifest itself physically. They may unconsciously clench their fists, tap their foot with impatience, or let out a loud sigh. These actions are the body's attempt to release some pent-up tension, like steam escaping from a boiling pot.

3. Emotional withdrawal

A person struggling with hidden anger may withdraw emotionally. They seem more distant as if they're watching life from behind a glass — visible to you but somehow out of reach. This distancing is a defensive tactic, a shield to protect their vulnerability.

Recognizing these indicators is the first step. Next, we want to understand the root of their anger. As we already know, anger is often a defense for deeper feelings — disappointment over a setback, fear of inadequacy, or grief over a loss. Anger acts as a fortress, protecting the more sensitive parts of a person's psyche from further harm.

Approach with empathy

If you see these signs, be kind and honest when you talk to your loved one. You don't want to blame them or say they're angry; you want to show that you've noticed a change and that you care. Let them know you're there and willing to listen when they're ready to talk.

Recognizing the subtle cues that our loved ones are angry allows us to comprehend the intricate emotions fueling their behavior. With this insight, we can assist them in validating their inner struggle without pressuring them to disclose more than they are comfortable with.

Achieving this balance can be difficult and involves love, patience, and a commitment to support them throughout their emotional journey.

Open hearts, safe words

Creating a safe place for honest conversation is like making a warm and welcoming campfire in the middle of our feelings. It's a place where warmth spreads, inviting even the most guarded hearts to come close, sit for a while, and share their stories without fear. To create this candid and welcoming atmosphere, try these strategies:

1. Choose the right moment

Timing is everything. Just as you wouldn't start a deep

conversation in the middle of a thunderstorm, choose a peaceful time to talk.

Avoid moments of high stress or when either of you is tired or distracted. Perhaps after dinner or during a quiet evening at home, when both of you feel relaxed, connected, and receptive.

2. Set the scene for comfort

The setting is key. Just as the glow of a campfire draws people together, a comfortable setting can encourage openness. Maybe it's a favorite corner of your home where you both feel relaxed. Minimize interruptions by silencing phones or turning off the TV. A candle or two can add a warm, inviting glow to the room.

3. Open with empathy

Begin the conversation with empathy and kindness, such as by offering a warm blanket to someone feeling cold. Use "I" statements to express yourself and avoid blame (chapter 5). For example, "*I've noticed that you've seemed a little distant lately, and I'm here if you want to talk about anything.*" This shows concern without pretending to know their feelings.

4. Listen more than you speak

Listening is the warmth that keeps the campfire burning. It means giving your full attention, nodding to show you're following, and refraining from interrupting or jumping to solutions. Being heard and understood is often all someone needs, rather than immediate advice.

5. Validate their feelings

Validation ignites the conversation, adding a spark like fuel to a fire. Acknowledge their feelings with phrases like, *"It sounds like that was really hard for you,"* or *"I can see why you're feeling that way."* Validation does not mean you agree, but it shows your respect for their perspective and emotions.

6. Make sure always to show respect

It's important to maintain a respectful tone during the dialogue. If things get heated, recommend a quick break to cool off and keep the conversation peaceful.

7. Ask open-ended questions to encourage sharing

If you want your loved one to open up, ask questions that require more than a one-word answer. Instead of asking, "Did that make you angry?" try, *"How did that situation make you feel?"* These questions gently nudge the conversation and spark further discussion.

8. Offer comfort

Finish the conversation with positive encouragement, like a cozy hug at the end of a campfire evening. Ensure they understand that you are there to support them, regardless of what they are experiencing.

"*I'm here for you, no matter what*" can be a powerful message of support and love.

Creating this space for open dialogue is about building trust and understanding in your relationship. After all, that's what we're all looking for.

Balancing empathy and boundaries

As a psychologist, I emphasize the importance of setting and maintaining clear boundaries while providing this support. Boundaries are necessary not only for your own mental and emotional well-being but also for the effectiveness of your support, just like sharing an umbrella in a storm protects you from getting wet.

Being there for your loved ones is important during difficult times without allowing their emotions to overwhelm you.

1. Understand boundaries

Think of boundaries as imperceptible lines that communicate to everyone the actions within the limits and those outside of them. Imagine having an invisible perimeter that tells others how close they can come without making you uncomfortable. "*I care about you and want to help, but there are some things I can and cannot do*" is what it means to set boundaries with someone who has anger problems.

2. Clearly express your boundaries

Talking about boundaries can be less intimidating than you think. It's like providing someone with a guide on how to be a supportive friend or partner.

You could say, *"I'm here to listen if you need to talk, but I can't be yelled at. We can chat when things are calmer."* it doesn't shut down communication; it guides it.

3. Know your limits

Admitting that you have limits is a healthy and essential aspect of self-awareness. Loving someone doesn't mean sacrificing your emotional well-being, just like enjoying the rain doesn't mean you have to get soaked. Consider what you can handle and determine where your limits lie. Maybe it's okay for you to listen without the pressure of always having the solutions.

4. Stick to your boundaries

If you only occasionally enforce your boundaries, it can send mixed signals and sabotage your efforts. Make it a habit to emphasize them, especially when your loved one challenges you, to create a sense of mutual respect.

5. Take care of yourself

Set aside time for self-care and ensure that your life does not revolve solely around your loved one's anger management. Taking space when needed is essential to setting boundaries. It doesn't mean you care less; it means you value your happiness and self-care.

6. Balance is key

When you're helping someone with anger issues, it's important to find a balance between supporting them and taking care of yourself. With clear boundaries, you can provide support without becoming overwhelmed. This is vital for maintaining the strength and patience required to support someone else.

7. Reach out for help if you need it

Supporting someone with anger issues can be isolating. Remember that a storm can damage even the best umbrellas. Seeking support for yourself, whether through a friend or a professional, is like repairing your umbrella to continue sharing it with others.

Establishing and upholding boundaries shows you value and respect yourself and your loved one. By doing so, you are heartily investing in the health and balance of your relationship. Constantly being on the receiving end of someone's anger can be draining and may lead to resentment.

Good boundaries help people with anger learn to take responsibility for their actions and emotions.

This is crucial for their personal growth and the development of healthy coping mechanisms. Now you know

Ramona Magyih

how boundaries help protect your relationship from becoming one-dimensional, centered only on anger issues.

Avoid these common mistakes

Good intentions don't always lead to the results we hope for. With that in mind, let's be proactive and talk about common mistakes that can hinder your ability to deal with anger so that you can enjoy the journey.

1. Unintentionally avoiding anger

Let's say you're trying to help an easily frustrated friend and unintentionally start avoiding anything that might upset them. It's like tiptoeing around a sleeping dragon; you do it out of concern, but it could mean the dragon never learns to control its fire. Instead, encourage open discussion of feelings and frustrations, offering support without shielding them from every possible trigger. The goal is to teach the dragon how to breathe fire safely, not to keep it asleep.

2. Sacrificing your own needs

It's wonderful to light the way for someone else, but imagine using your last match to brighten another's path, only to find yourself left in the dark.

You cannot guide someone through the shadows if your light has gone out.

Remember to nurture your heart with the things that

bring you joy and peace, whether through quiet relaxation, engaging in your favorite hobbies, or cherishing time with friends. This isn't selfish — it's essential. You're kindling your light, glowing from within, to continue brightening the lives of those you hold dear.

3. Avoiding difficult conversations

Sometimes, you may shy away from talking about difficult things out of a desire not to upset anyone. But imagine if every time you went hiking and saw a sign for a steep trail, you took the flat route instead. You'd be missing out on some fantastic views. Approaching tough conversations with kindness and empathy can lead to breakthroughs and greater understanding. Taking the scenic route, knowing it may be difficult, but believing that the view at the top is worth it.

4. Trying to fix everything

When someone we care about is struggling, our first instinct may be to step in and fix everything for them. But imagine you're on that hike together, carrying them every time they stumble. They may never learn to navigate the tricky trails on their own. Help them back up, but give them the space to steady their steps. **Be a guide, not a bearer.**

5. Losing sight of the journey

When trying to help someone control anger, we often focus too much on the end goal of finding peace and calm and forget to appreciate the process along the way. The journey of growth and change takes time, but there are still precious moments to cherish along the way. Appreciate every bit of progress and savor the journey instead of focusing solely on the end goal.

By keeping these pitfalls in mind, you can guide your loved one to better anger management, ensuring your boundaries remain intact. To succeed together, you need to find harmony in providing support, taking care of yourself, guiding without dominating, and embracing learning opportunities. By being aware of each step we take, we can avoid obstacles and create a fulfilling journey full of understanding, growth, and joyful moments.

Helping loved one's checklist

The next step is to apply what we've learned about supporting our loved ones and prepare ourselves with the right tools. I have a list of exercises and questions to help you be more effective in this role. You're welcome to revisit the earlier chapters for a quick refresher. These tools are simple but can be incredibly powerful once implemented. I use them with my clients, and they've proven highly effective.

1. How has your understanding of anger changed?
Reflect on your newfound insights about anger from a

supportive perspective. How does understanding the reasons behind a loved one's anger change how you communicate with them?

2. What support strategies work best?

Think back to a time when you tried to calm a loved one during an argument. Which approaches seemed to defuse the tension, and which fell flat? It's like identifying which tools in your backpack can help you navigate through thick underbrush.

3. How do you identify their triggers?

Identifying what triggers your loved one's anger can be challenging. Have you noticed any consistent patterns or triggers? Being aware of these can help you better anticipate and manage potential conflicts. For detailed insights into triggers, review Chapter 2.

4. How can you communicate more effectively?

I cannot emphasize enough the value of clear, compassionate communication. Reflect on a time when your well-meaning efforts to offer support were met with confusion and misunderstanding. Next time, consider improving your approach to ensure your intentions are clear and your support is genuinely felt. Chapter 5 has some great insights into assertive communication.

Healing support exercises

1. Emotional mapping

Work with your loved one to create an emotional "map" if they're open to the idea. This can help you better understand the landscape and plan routes to avoid potential pitfalls. If you want a more in-depth understanding, I recommend reviewing Chapter 9 and using the guided journey workbook I've thoughtfully created.

2. The supportive pause

When faced with your loved one's anger, try giving yourself a moment to pause and consider your response. Taking a moment to breathe or walking away to collect your thoughts might help. Just like you wouldn't go into a storm without a raincoat, it's crucial to take precautions before rushing into things. Take some time to review Chapter 4, where you'll find simple techniques.

3. Role-playing for empathy

Role-playing exercises where participants switch positions and perspectives can enhance the learning experience. Take on the role of the angry person while your partner attempts to respond. This role reversal can offer a fresh perspective on how each of you interprets and reacts to emotions, creating a deeper understanding of one another's experiences (and that is empathy).

Go through Chapter 9 for more information on the emotional game.

4. Daily debriefs

Make it a habit to have regular daily conversations and check-ins with one another. Share what went well and what didn't, and express gratitude for help and effort. It's like telling the most memorable and challenging moments of the day by the campfire, creating a deeper sense of connection.

When you incorporate these reflective practices into your support plan, you can assist your loved one with anger management while building a stronger relationship and gaining a deeper understanding. Overcoming someone's anger is a shared ride for both of you. It takes patience, understanding, and a willingness to learn and adapt. Let's start this journey with a positive attitude, prepared to overcome challenges and celebrate achievements.

You are amazing! I appreciate you for being so patient and loving.

As we close this chapter, take a moment to look back on the journey we've been on together. Supporting a loved one during an emotional storm isn't a walk in the park. This adventure has twists and turns, ups and downs, and unpredictable weather. But hey, aren't the challenging parts of any great adventure what makes it more exciting?

This journey is about more than just helping someone deal with their anger. It is a path that leads through the dense forests of emotion and across the open fields of understanding. Along the way, you will both discover deeper connections, new insights into each other's hearts, and the love that can only come from facing problems together.

CALM WATERS

12. Anger Displays

As we come close to the end of our anger management journey, let's take a moment to reflect on our findings and acknowledge the effort and progress we've made. We explored the nature of our reactions, identified triggers, unpacked the psychology behind anger, learned the best responses and exercises for improvement, and gained insights into recognizing and dealing with anger.

Now that we have a solid foundation, it is time to add more in-depth knowledge. In my work as a psychologist specializing in emotional healing, I've seen how transformative it can be when individuals recognize and understand their anger patterns and those of others. This is the first step toward managing it effectively. Anger can manifest as passive aggression, open aggression, or assertive anger, each with its own set of behaviors and consequences. Recognizing different anger expressions in others can profoundly improve your relationships.

When you understand how someone else expresses fury, you can respond with empathy and patience rather than reacting with your anger.

Passive aggression: The silent alarm

Imagine someone baking you a cake but leaving you to clean up the kitchen mess while declaring, "Oh, I did it all for you!" That's passive aggression, the silent alarm of anger. It's like feeling angry, but instead of expressing it openly, it's conveyed through subtle actions.

Characteristics

This type of anger sneaks around corners. It may appear as deliberate forgetfulness or procrastination, backhanded compliments or subtle insults, sarcasm or cynicism, or giving someone the silent treatment. It's like saying, "I'm fine," when there's a storm boiling inside.

Sources of this type of anger expression

- *Fear of confrontation*

Passive-aggressive people often avoid confrontation or conflict because they fear it. This anxiety may be rooted in past experiences where expressing anger led to negative outcomes or from being raised in environments that discouraged or punished anger expression, just like Jamie, who, as a child, often witnessed heated arguments between her parents, which sometimes escalated into shouting matches. Wanting to avoid conflict, Jamie learned to keep her frustrations to herself, fearing that expressing disagreement might lead to similar disputes.

As she grew up, Jamie's avoidance of confrontation manifested as passive-aggressive behavior because the direct expression of anger felt too dangerous and uncomfortable.

* *Feelings of powerlessness*

When people feel they lack control over their situation, they might use subtle ways to convey their dissatisfaction or claim their authority when they feel powerless or underappreciated. Like Brad, who grew up in a household where strict obedience was demanded, and any dissent was harshly punished. Whenever he felt upset or mistreated, his parents dismissed his feelings, telling him to "toughen up" and stop complaining. This constant invalidation made him feel powerless and unable to influence his environment positively. In response, Brad developed passive-aggressive behaviors, such as procrastination and intentional inefficiency, as subtle ways to exert control without openly challenging authority.

- *Avoiding responsibility*

Passive aggression is a tactic for avoiding responsibility for one's feelings and actions. Aggressive people have mastered the art of conveying their displeasure indirectly, skillfully masking their anger behind a veneer of politeness or disinterest.

Think of Mara, the youngest child in her family, who was often babied by her parents, who did not expect her to take responsibility for chores or decisions. Whenever something went wrong, her siblings or parents would fix the situation. This lack of accountability taught Mara to avoid taking responsibility for her actions and emotions, leading to passive-aggressive behaviors in adulthood, where she would express her displeasure indirectly, never fully owning up to her feelings or behaviors.

Dealing with passive aggression

Look for a hidden message. What is not being said directly? Recognize the signs of passive aggression and address them directly.

For example, if someone is consistently late as a way to express their displeasure, discuss the issue openly. Create a safe environment for the person to express their feelings openly and directly.

This might involve reassurances that their opinions are valued and that conflict, when handled respectfully, is healthy. Chapter 5 offers simple techniques to encourage open communication.

Open aggression: The thunderstorm

Now, think of someone who yells or slams doors when angry. That's open aggression — a storm of anger. It's unmistakable and signals to everyone that a storm is happening.

Characteristics

This kind of anger is impossible to miss. It's characterized by yelling, swearing, throwing or breaking objects, or physical violence. This type of aggression can be highly destructive to relationships and is often the most visible and stigmatized form of anger. It's as if the person is broadcasting, "*I'm angry!*"

Sources of this kind of anger expression

• *Learned behavior*

Aggressive behavior can be learned from essential individuals in a person's life, like parents, friends, or influencers. When people witness aggression being rewarded or considered normal, they might start thinking it's okay to respond violently in the same way.

Meet James, who grew up in a neighborhood where displays of aggression were common and often seen as a means to resolve disputes or assert dominance. His role models, including older siblings and friends, frequently resolved their frustrations through verbal threats or physical fights. Observing these behaviors, James learned to replicate them, perceiving open aggression as a usual and effective way to express anger and achieve respect.

• *Impulse control issues*

Biological factors, including difficulties with impulse control, can lead to open aggression. This might involve neurological issues where the brain's mechanisms for regulating emotions and impulses are less effective, leading to more explosive and uncontrollable expressions of anger.

For example, when the prefrontal cortex is not functioning optimally — due to genetic factors, injury, or developmental issues — it can lead to diminished control over impulses and poor judgment, which may manifest as open aggression.

An overactive amygdala can cause heightened emotional reactions and a quick escalation to aggression.

Low levels of serotonin have been associated with increased aggression, impulsivity, and a lower threshold for anger. Meanwhile, dopamine regulation issues can affect reward-seeking behavior and risk assessment, potentially leading to aggressive outbursts. Deficiencies or dysfunctions in gamma-aminobutyric acid signaling can reduce the brain's ability to inhibit aggressive responses effectively. Elevated testosterone levels can increase tendencies towards dominance and aggression, affecting how individuals respond to provocations or perceived threats.

Traumatic brain injury and neurological and mental health disorders can impact brain function and, consequently, impulse control.

Let's meet Olivia, who showed signs of ADHD from a young age, characterized by difficulty concentrating, hyperactivity, and impulsive behavior. Her impulsivity made it hard for her to control her reactions or think through the consequences of her actions. This often resulted in sudden outbursts of anger in situations where she felt overwhelmed or unable to cope, as she lacked the tools to manage her immediate emotional response.

- *High levels of distress*

People under high emotional stress or pressure may have a lower tolerance for frustration, resulting in more frequent and intense outbursts of aggression. Allow me to give you a brief overview.

Intense stress changes the brain chemistry and consumes significant cognitive resources, focusing the brain's attention on perceived threats and problem-solving related to the source of stress.

This concentration can lead to mental overload, where the brain has less capacity to deal with additional stimuli or minor annoyances — with the brain's resources stretched thin, there's less capacity for emotional regulation, which is crucial in managing reactions to frustration. The consequences can be a shorter temper, heightened emotional sensitivity, and a greater susceptibility to irritation and frustration.

Just like Daniel, whose parents divorced when he was eight, an event led to significant changes in his life, including moving to a new city and changing schools. The stress of these changes, coupled with the ongoing conflict between his parents, left him in a constant state of emotional distress. This heightened anxiety and insecurity significantly lowered his threshold for frustration, making him quick to anger over minor issues that worsened his sense of instability.

Managing open aggression

If this is how you express anger, you need to discover safe outlets for intense feelings. Practice cooling down before discussing issues with the strategies in Chapter 8.

Or if the situation you are in escalates to potential violence with someone else, it's important to remove yourself from the immediate environment. Use calm, non-confrontational language and non-threatening body expression. Speak slowly and maintain a steady voice to help calm the situation. Clearly state the consequences if aggressive behavior continues. Boundaries are crucial to protecting yourself, and letting the aggressive person know their behavior is unacceptable.

These stories emphasize how childhood experiences shape our anger expression styles. Whether you display passive or open aggression, understanding these childhood roots can be the first step toward healthier anger management strategies. Self-discovery, patience, compassion, courage, and therapy can help you explore these early experiences and learn new, more constructive ways to handle your temper.

Assertive anger: The clear sky after rain

Assertive anger is the healthiest form of anger expression. Imagine someone calmly explaining why they are upset and offering feasible solutions. This is assertive anger, the clear sky after a storm. It's about sharing your feelings openly and respectfully without overshadowing others.

Characteristics

Assertive anger is like a calm conversation in the middle of a storm. It involves saying what you feel and why, but in a way that respects everyone involved. It's like saying, *"If you do X, it makes me feel Y. Can we try Z instead?"* Assertive anger is heartfelt and straightforward but also respectful and controlled.

Sources of assertive anger

- *Childhood*

Assertive anger often comes from a healthy emotional upbringing, where children are taught to express their emotions clearly and respectfully. In such environments, individuals learn early that it's possible to express anger in ways that are constructive and non-damaging to others. Discussions about emotions are a regular part of family life, and adults model assertive communication by expressing their feelings clearly and listening to each other.

- *Emotional intelligence*

High levels of emotional intelligence contribute to assertive anger because they mean being able to recognize and handle one's own emotions and the emotions of others. It involves realizing that our behavior influences others, and we need to adjust it more to ensure effective and empathetic communication.

- *Self-awareness and Self-regulation*

People who express anger assertively are typically more aware of their emotional triggers and have developed strategies to manage their reactions to maintain control over their anger. First, they recognize when they feel frustrated or irritated. Then, they assess why they feel this way and decide how best to address the situation. Through deep breathing and open discussions about their feelings, they skillfully handle their emotions, ensuring their anger is expressed positively and constructively.

Why is it healthy? This anger display honors both your feelings and those of the other person. It leads to greater understanding, solutions, and, in many cases, stronger relationships. It's a strategy for directing the inner storm toward a peaceful resolution.

Embracing assertive anger

Cultivate effective and polite communication by clearly stating your needs without offending others. If you want additional information, review the previous chapters.

Be aware of your anger triggers and your typical responses. This level of awareness can assist you in responding assertively instead of impulsively. Show that you are listening to the other party and consider their perspective. This encourages a respectful and constructive dialogue. Focus on finding solutions rather than dwelling on the problem. This approach fosters cooperation and mutual respect.

Anger, in all its manifestations, is part of the human experience. Learning to manage and express it effectively is like learning to sail in shifting seas. Whether you are dealing with silent alarms, thunderstorms, or striving for clear skies, understanding these displays of anger can help you handle your emotional state more effectively.

This journey is not always easy, but it's worth every

step. Embrace this understanding, and let it guide you to a place of emotional well-being and deeper connections with those around you.

Guide this fiery passion

Let's explore how we can use assertive anger principles to create masterpieces from our interactions and relationships.

Blend the shades.

It's human to feel shades of passive or open aggression. Acknowledge these emotions and then think about how to blend them into the more balanced approach of assertive anger. It's about channeling the raw energy of your feelings into something that is both thoughtful and constructive.

Draw with compassion.

Frame your responses to anger with compassion for yourself and others. Understand that mastering anger is a lifelong process of learning, growth, and occasional mistakes. Anger is a part of who you are, but your reactions gain depth and purpose with each level of awareness. Keep making small changes, even if some are more difficult.

Paint with patience.

Handle every situation with the same level of patience that an artist would have while seeking the perfect light. Patience helps you understand and connect with others by letting you experience various emotions and respond thoughtfully.

Frame it with forgiveness.

Start by forgiving yourself and others for not always handling anger well. Make a promise to move forward with empathy and a desire to learn and improve.

Think of anger as a palette of colors, each shade representing a unique expression of anger in our lives. There are the cool, reserved blues and purples of passive aggression, where emotions lurk beneath the surface, suggested more by actions than words. It's like the chill of an early morning frost, where discomfort is palpable but not openly expressed.

Then there are the fiery reds and oranges of outright aggression, vivid and impossible to miss. This anger bursts forth without reservation, like the sound and fury of a summer thunderstorm. It's loud and clear, and while it can be intimidating, it's also sincere.

But one color stands out for its balance and harmony: the calm greens and soft golds of assertive anger. This color evokes the vitality and hope of a forest at dawn. It symbolizes anger that understands its force and chooses to channel it positively, valuing transparent, sincere conversation to resolve conflicts and enhance understanding. What colors represent your anger? Can you paint it? Let this be a visual representation of your anger and a gentle nudge to focus on inner healing.

BE KIND TO YOURSELF

As we end this journey together, I just wanted to take a moment to reflect on what we've learned and how you can use these lessons in your everyday life. Managing anger is an ongoing process, but the right tools and mindset can lead to positive changes. Here are three key takeaways I hope you remember as you move forward.

Anger is a natural emotion with a purpose

First and foremost, remember that anger is not something to be afraid of or pushed aside but rather understood and channeled. Anger lets us know when something isn't right — when our boundaries are crossed, injustices occur, or our needs aren't being met. Recognizing this helps us see anger as a warning rather than a problem.

Think of anger as your internal alarm system that signals potential danger and indicates that something needs your attention. The key is listening to this alarm and responding thoughtfully rather than impulsively. You can use the techniques we've discussed, like deep breathing, the 10-second pause, and assertive communication, to channel this powerful emotion into positive action.

Patience and practice lead to progress

Managing anger isn't something that can be fixed overnight. It's a journey that requires compassion, self-discovery, courage, patience, and practice. It's okay to feel frustrated if you don't see immediate results but remember, every small step counts. Celebrate the small victories — when you successfully use a calming technique or choose to respond rather than react, you're making progress.

Imagine you're learning a new skill, like playing an instrument or running a marathon. It takes time, effort, and consistent practice. The same goes for managing anger. By sticking with it, you'll gradually notice changes in how you handle situations that used to trigger you. Keep practicing the strategies you've learned; over time, you'll build a more resilient, skillful approach to anger.

Improving your anger management skills can bring you closer and happier relationships and, thus, better overall well-being.

Managing anger leads to closer relationships with your loved ones.

Finally, when you learn to manage your anger, you're not just keeping the peace — you're building healthier, more fulfilling connections with the people around you. Good anger management helps you communicate more clearly, set and respect boundaries, and resolve conflicts constructively.

Think about how this impacts your relationships with family, friends, and colleagues.

When you handle anger well, you create an environment of trust and respect. This makes people feel safer and more connected to you.

How does it make you feel? Your answer will be your motivation.

Keep making progress

As you continue your journey, keep these key takeaways in mind, and remember that this book is only the beginning. The real work happens in your daily life as you apply these principles and strategies. Take it one day at a time, and don't be too hard on yourself. Every effort you make is a step toward a calmer, more empowered you.

Thank you for joining me on this journey. I hope you find the tools and insights we've explored to be valuable as you move forward. Here's to a future filled with understanding, growth, and positive transformation.

My deepest wish is to help emotionally burdened people reconnect with themselves and lighten their heavy hearts. Exciting things are coming — more books providing easy tools for emotional well-being.

About the Author

Ramona Magyih is a psychologist and neuroscience fanatic specializing in emotional well-being and a mental wellness advocate.

Losing both her parents when she was young left her feeling lost and disconnected. She struggled to express her emotions and deal with the grief. That's why she became a psychologist — she wanted to understand herself better, heal, and help others avoid being stuck in pain. For years, she was helping others but forgot about herself. While training teams and individuals to reach their peak performance and be emotionally well, she also realized she needed to heal. So, she went to therapy and reconnected with her buried feelings and past trauma.

By focusing on her emotional healing, she learned how to manage intense feelings, heal emotional numbness, and support overall well-being to navigate the ups and downs of life. Her interest in brain chemistry grew, making her a neuroscience enthusiast eager to learn about the brain's inner workings to improve therapy effectiveness. Positive psychology has given her valuable insights into the profound effects of our mindset on overall life quality. Motivated by curiosity, she delved into the world of psychotherapy techniques and mindfulness, eager to understand how we can effectively address and nurture emotional well-being in our society. Using all her experience and knowledge, she now helps others to heal and reconnect with their feelings and selves.

She doesn't like things to be complicated, so she loves to break down psychology concepts and techniques into easy-to-understand steps. Her goal? To share the tools you need to improve your emotional intelligence, build self-awareness, and boost your confidence, all in a way that empowers and sparks a new you in real life.

 Her blog and social posts are dedicated to sharing her insights on emotional healing. She reveals the masks we wear to hide our scars, inner wounds, and ways to heal.

This is her first book, written to be insightful and valuable in your journey. Join her community to discover the strength that comes from healing and the freedom we find in connecting deeply with ourselves and others.

Bibliography

1. "Anger: Wisdom for Cooling the Flames" by Thich Nhat Hanh
2. "The Dance of Anger: A Woman's Guide to Changing the Patterns of Intimate Relationships" by Harriet Lerner
3. "Rage: A Step-by-Step Guide to Overcoming Explosive Anger" by Ronald Potter-Efron
4. "The Cow in the Parking Lot: A Zen Approach to Overcoming Anger" by Leonard Scheff and Susan Edmiston
5. "Healing the Angry Brain: How Understanding the Way Your Brain Works Can Help You Control Anger and Aggression" by Ronald Potter-Efron
6. "The Surprising Purpose of Anger: Beyond Anger Management: Finding the Gift" by Marshall B. Rosenberg

7. "When Anger Hurts: Quieting the Storm Within" by Matthew McKay, Peter D. Rogers, and Judith McKay

8. "Anger Management for Dummies" by Charles H. Elliott and Laura L. Smith

9. "Angry All the Time: An Emergency Guide to Anger Control" by Ronald T. Potter-Efron

10. "Overcoming Emotions that Destroy: Practical Help for Those Angry Feelings That Ruin Relationships" by Chip Ingram and Becca Johnson

11. "The Anger Trap: Free Yourself from the Frustrations that Sabotage Your Life" by Les Carter

12. "Letting Go of Anger: The Eleven Most Common Anger Styles and What to Do About Them" by Ronald T. Potter-Efron and Patricia S. Potter-Efron

13. "Taking Charge of Anger: How to Resolve Conflict, Sustain Relationships, and Express Yourself without Losing Control" by W. Robert Nay

14. "The Gift of Anger: Seven Steps to Uncover the Meaning of Anger and Gain Awareness, True Strength, and Peace" by Marcia Cannon

15. "Anger: Taming a Powerful Emotion" by Gary Chapman

16. "How to Keep People from Pushing Your Buttons" by Albert Ellis and Arthur Lange

17. "The Explosive Child: A New Approach for Understanding and Parenting Easily Frustrated, Chronically Inflexible Children" by Ross W. Greene

18. "Your Defiant Child: Eight Steps to Better Behavior" by Russell A. Barkley and Christine M. Benton

19. "Calming the Emotional Storm: Using Dialectical Behavior Therapy Skills to Manage Your Emotions and Balance Your Life" by Sheri Van Dijk

20. "Beyond Anger: A Guide for Men: How to Free Yourself from the Grip of Anger and Get More Out of Life" by Thomas J. Harbin

21. "Emotional Agility: Get Unstuck, Embrace Change, and Thrive in Work and Life" by Susan David

22. "Buddha's Brain: The Practical Neuroscience of Happiness, Love, and Wisdom" by Rick Hanson with Richard Mendius

23. "The Happiness Hypothesis" by Jonathan Haidt

24. "Descartes' Error" by Antonio Damasio

25. "The Blank Slate" by Steven Pinker

26. "Consilience" by Edward O Wilson

27. "Working With Emotional Intelligence" by Daniel Goleman

28. "Destructive Emotions: How Can We Overcome Them?" by Daniel Goleman

29. "Emotional Intelligence 2.0" by Travis Bradberry and Jean Greaves

30. "Atlas of the Heart: Mapping Meaningful Connection and the Language of Human Experience" by Brené Brown

Don't shout, speak

Made in United States
Orlando, FL
12 September 2024

51446907R00117